Conscious Impact

Praise for Conscious Impact

"This book masterfully bridges the worlds of business leadership and contemplative wisdom, offering a practical 6-week roadmap for leaders seeking to effectively impact our complex and often frustrating world."

Christiana Figueres, Co-founder of Global Optimism, Executive Secretary of the UN Framework Convention on Climate Change 2010-2016, co-author of *The Future We Choose*

"Leading a company as a CEO in today's unpredictable world demands a great deal of care—both for yourself and for those around you. Staying mentally strong and aligned with your personal values is key and a skill that can be cultivated. Susanne's new book is the ideal practical guide for any leader looking to embark on the journey toward 'mindful leadership'."

Sabine Busse, CEO Hager Group

"In times of turmoil and confusion, changing the way we go forward is much more about the 'how' than the 'what'. This book gives a comprehensive approach and good hints for so many people feeling lost. It addresses the current emptiness of the word 'leadership' by emphasizing that it is, first and foremost, a journey in the company of others towards humility and courage."

Carlos Alvarez Pereira, Secretary General of The Club of Rome

"What's gotten leaders here will not get them to the 'there' the world needs now. ***Conscious Impact*** *delivers the expanded toolkit modern leaders need to navigate the shifting terrain of creating impact and building success for the journey ahead. Through vivid stories, clear images, and thoughtful exercises, Dr. von der Becke maps the path—and guides the mindsets—for bringing true humanity to the role of leadership. It's a one-stop handbook to the essential changes shaping leadership excellence as we face the future."*

Ellen Petry Leanse, Neuroscience Educator, Life Impact Coach, and Author of *The Happiness Hack*

"Susanne offers wise and helpful perspectives and practices for leaders in this challenging time."

Jack Kornfield, Author of *A Path With Heart*

"The perilous times we are witnessing require an evolutionary step up by leaders everywhere. We clearly will not build a flourishing world for people and planet by using the same extractive and destructive logic that has become mainstream. ***Conscious Impact*** *gets straight to this evolutionary need by embedding the business acumen and existential awareness that are Susanne von der Becke's hallmarks. Few authors truly understand both worlds the way she does. I strongly recommend not only reading it, but using it frequently as a source of knowledge and wisdom for the challenging years ahead."*

Marcello Palazzi, Entrepreneur for human progress, Co-Founder & Executive Chair, Leaders for Good; Co-Founder, B Lab Europe

"Many conscious leaders, including myself, are convinced that systems change does not happen without inner transformation, without a mindset shift within ourselves, our organizations, and the people we work with. I refer to this as 'mindset shift for systems change' or 'cosmic dance between inner and outer transformation'. Susanne has created a compelling and inspiring book for business leaders, who want to explore this dance, who have decided to cultivate clarity, resiliency, and heartfulness—necessary ingredients for leading, co-creating, and co-envisioning our future. In the book, Susanne is offering a practical toolbox, including guided meditations, various breath exercises, meaningful questions, and insightful nudges for reflections—accessible to beginners as well as experienced practitioners. This is a must read for any business leader, who has the desire and intention to co-create the biggest transformation humanity has ever experienced, the transformation from an extractive economic and financial system to a regenerative one."

Charly Kleissner PhD, Co-Founder Toniic, TWIST, and the KL Felicitas Foundation; full member of the Club of Rome

Conscious Impact

Mindful Leadership for Meaningful Change

Susanne von der Becke

tp

Triarchy Press

Published in this First Edition in 2025 by:
Triarchy Press
Axminster, England

info@triarchypress.net
www.triarchypress.net

A catalogue record for this book is available from the British Library.

Cover design and illustration: from an idea by Chris Binding
Breathwork illustrations (pp. 51, 75, 151): copyright © Michèle Imhof

Print ISBN: 978-1-917251-10-5
ePub ISBN: 978-1-917251-11-2

Contents

INTRODUCTION

As business leaders we tend to see opportunities where others don't, fix problems as they arise, and see the glass as half full rather than half empty; yet these times can still feel overwhelming and exhausting. Our nervous system is on constant alert as we receive news and personal and business communications across multiple channels: emails, apps, and platforms. The world is moving from one big crisis to the next, making planning more difficult, and outcomes more uncertain. Time seems to run faster than usual, and we never seem to have enough of it. No matter how much we improve our efficiency and time management, the to-do lists seem to magically refill themselves, leaving us feeling always a little behind while doing our best to juggle multiple projects and responsibilities at work and home.

If you've found yourself in this state, perhaps you have tried meditation to help you relax, improve your concentration, and boost your health. Over the past years, meditation and mindfulness have seen a huge surge in popularity, which is both a testimony to the power of these ancient practices and the need of our times. Many business leaders whom I meet through various networks tell me that starting a meditation or mindfulness practice has shifted the needle in their performance. This is great but the impact of those practices can be even more transformative.

The crises we are currently experiencing, environmental destruction, war and violence, social injustices, mental and physical health problems, are opportunities to reconnect with what truly matters to us. Rather than improving your performance in a broken system, mindfulness and meditation can help you tap into the insight that enables you to see ways to change the system. This happens because your inner and outer work are connected: inner change enables and motivates the outer change of processes, systems, and organizations that you lead, which in turn strengthens the inner change in people impacted by those processes, systems, and institutions. Your leadership does not stop at work, it starts with yourself and determines how you are with the people around you, including your family and community.

At this critical time in history, business leaders are in both a sweet and a hard spot. On the one hand, the outdated rules of short-termism and profit-maximization of many of our old systems can limit our ability to create positive impact on people and nature. On the other hand, businesses are the heart of the economy which puts their leaders in a unique position to influence the rules of the game and to create positive impact within and through our organizations.

However, when I talk about our role as leaders, I am not referring to a title or position of power. I am talking about our ability to inspire others and our commitment to take responsibility for the impact that our actions have on ourselves, the people around us, and the planet. Our legacy as leaders will not only be defined by the size and profitability of our organizations but also by the extent to which we have contributed to finding solutions to our most pressing environmental and social challenges. Some of us have already started to make changes in our organizations but feel like our efforts are just a drop in the ocean. Some of us have bowed to the public pressure to be seen as more sustainable and taken some tentative steps—but we know those changes are superficial at best. And some of us are so busy with the everyday challenges of work and life that the idea of saving the world seems very far from what we are actually able to do.

No matter where you are on your impact journey—whether you are a small business entrepreneur or run a big company, and whether you consider yourself a leader or not (I've met many people, especially women, who are pioneers in their field but hesitate to identify as leaders)—each one of us is a piece of the puzzle in the emerging future. We are all needed and can all be a force for good, right now. For each of us, the journey of creating positive change starts within and finds expression through our actions.

Caring for ourselves and caring for our world are connected. Every action begins with an inner process we may or may not be aware of. The root cause of our crises is our sense of disconnection from within ourselves, each other, and from nature. When we learn to become aware of—and able to influence—our inner world, we can reconnect both within and around us and create conscious impact. As we learn to create the change we want to see from a place of love rather than fear, we can connect with an inner spaciousness from which new solutions will emerge.

This book will guide you to establish an inner work practice in six weeks so that you can create the change you want to see, for yourself, and the world around you. The teachings, stories, practices, and reflections that I share are designed to help you develop the leadership skills that will help you see how your current thinking and actions contribute to the problems you are trying to solve. The mindfulness practices in this book are designed to strengthen your wellbeing and develop your capacity to move from automatic reaction to conscious response. This way, you can start creating impact and create action from a deep sense of connection—within yourself, with others, and with nature.

How to use this book

Unlike most of my teachers, I am not a monk. My practice integrates the wisdom from these teachings into the realities and challenges of daily life. When I am not writing, teaching, or meditating, I enjoy learning from changemakers and business leaders, many of whom I have met in my former role as chair of an environmental forum, or in my capacity as an investor, board member, and business owner. Being married to an entrepreneur keeps me real. I like to think about the big picture, to discuss concepts and frameworks. When I say that our inner and outer worlds are connected, my husband asks me, "Yes, but what does it mean, practically?" Therefore, as we go through each chapter and mindfulness practice, I aim to show you how your inner work is directly linked to the outer issues we want to address and help you regain a sense of agency.

Mindfulness goes back centuries and has only recently become somewhat fashionable as renowned Buddhist teachers such as Jack Kornfield, Joseph Goldstein, Jon Kabat-Zinn, Sharon Salzberg, and others brought these practices and teachings to the West. However, the mindfulness-based practices I share in this book are universal: and they work if you are Christian, Jewish, Muslim, Hindu, or nonreligious. You don't have to believe in anything to experience the benefits of mindfulness and for it to help you create change from within. Wherever possible and helpful, I will share with you the latest scientific findings on how different meditation practices change our brain and body.

Sometimes, mindfulness is understood as simply bringing awareness to our present-moment experience. There is, however, much more going on than that. We practice being aware of our present-moment experience without clinging or rejecting through our judging mind and holding our experience with a sense of curiosity and kindness. The purpose is to develop self-understanding and wisdom that helps us choose the right action in a given situation. With practice, we become better able to choose a deliberate response over a habitual reaction and act in alignment with what truly matters to us.

Meditation is the formal part of the practice, where we can reside in a 'laboratory-style setting' that allows us to tap into deeper states of concentration, insight, and regeneration. It is the place where we train for the everyday challenges of being human and where we get to experience a sense of connection and wholeness that is so easily forgotten as we go about our day.

The book is structured as a six-week program, where each week builds on the last. Each week includes:

1. A theoretical introduction to the week's topic, including stories from other business leaders and insights from my practice, followed by a 'Going Deeper' section on a specific aspect of the topic.
2. Exercises and reflections to integrate insights from your own experience into your daily life and work
3. A daily guided meditation practice accessible on your phone or device and optional breathwork to support your practice.

The meditation practice builds a lasting foundation to help you collect the mind, investigate the mind, and move from autopilot to deliberate and wise action. The breathwork is a more immediate instrument to influence your nervous system and corresponding physical and emotional states. My intention is to provide you with a toolkit to experiment with and see what works best for you.

The exercises help integrate mindfulness into your work and daily life. I suggest you choose 1-2 questions and 1-2 exercises to focus on each week. I have intentionally provided a variety so you can explore what feels most helpful to you in the moment. The book is meant to be a resource you can revisit. While reading it sequentially is beneficial at first, you can later return to specific chapters, questions, exercises, meditations, and breathwork to support you through different phases of your life and journey as a changemaker.

My recommendation is that you follow the order of the book because it is designed to gradually build your mindfulness practice. The book is divided into two Parts. Part One explores the context of our outer and inner crises as a symptom of our larger disconnection, and why addressing these complex challenges requires new leadership skills. Part Two guides you in establishing your mindfulness practice to develop six core leadership skills, working at the level of the body, mind, and heart. The book finishes with recommendations for where to go from here and how to continue your journey of caring for your inner and outer world.

A piece of the puzzle

I was still a child when I first declared, "I am going to make the world a better place!" My father was a journalist, so I grew up watching and hearing the news. Even then, the news was primarily reporting the doom and gloom of the times, and I felt a strong sense of responsibility to do something about it. Of course, I had no idea how to achieve this, and the adult world often reacted with skepticism, wondering, "Who does she think she is?" and "Does she think she's something special?"

No, I did not think I was special; I thought that everyone was, and I still do. I believe that each one of us has a unique role to play in creating the world we long to see. At the time, I felt an uncomfortable sense of shame about wanting to do good. And I still hear executives tell me about similar reactions they get when they first challenge the status quo and want to implement more environmentally or people-friendly policies. It takes courage to do things differently. With an inner practice, we can turn difficulty into strength and when we get triggered into feeling naïve, not powerful enough, or whatever it may be, we can look inside and work with it. But I did not know that as a child.

I have been interested in inner work, like healing and meditation, since my early twenties, but for a long time, this part of me was separate from my professional life. It often felt like I had to choose between seeking inner peace and creating outer impact in the world. As a student of management at the London School of Economics, I wrote my master's thesis on corporate social responsibility, even though it wasn't part of my curriculum. In my circles, this was not a popular topic. Twenty-three years ago, when I wrote my thesis, Corporate Social Responsibility was far from mainstream; if companies had a CSR policy, it was usually because of external pressure, and it was definitely not mainstream then.

Making money was popular. It was also an entirely practical objective if you wanted to be financially independent. I found it thrilling to be working on the trading floor at Lehman Brothers, with its long hours, work-hard play-hard mentality, and highly competitive environment. My role in structured finance, selling asset-backed securities and collateralized debt obligations, allowed me to achieve financial independence and put me right in the eye of the storm which would later trigger the Global Financial Crisis of 2008. It was this experience that made me aware of the fact that our financial system had lost sight of its purpose—to support the economy and economic innovation. Instead of serving the economy, it had started mostly serving itself, making money from making money.

When I left Lehman Brothers it was neither due to a sudden burst of wisdom nor a premonition of its future collapse. It was the decision to follow my heart and move to Switzerland, where I would be with my now-husband. Lehman Brothers declared bankruptcy on 15th September 2008, and the entire financial system unraveled. What followed was the biggest economic downturn since the Great Depression. By then, I was working for a fund of hedge funds and private equity, and I was deeply moved by the suffering that was unleashed in the economy while financial institutions were rescued through state and central bank interventions.

I was curious to understand how the failure of a relatively small investment bank could trigger a market meltdown of such scale and embarked on a PhD investigating financial crises. It was during this time that I was first introduced to complex systems thinking. Complex systems are more than the sum of their parts and their interconnected and fractal nature, directly observable from the outside, resonated deeply with my inner observations during meditation.

Maintaining a regular meditation practice proved unexpectedly useful while I pursued my PhD. Whenever I felt overwhelmed or stuck in my analysis, I would take a moment to sit quietly. I would gather all the data and then sit with the confusion, not try to solve it, and let myself become empty. Not empty in the sense of having no thoughts, which is impossible, but empty in the sense of having no judgment and no preconception. Being in nature and doing something completely different, with joy and ease, also helped clear my mind. And in this way, without doing anything else, a new perspective would usually emerge that would lead me to my next step. I still practice this today whenever I don't know a solution to a problem or what to do next. It is a humbling and beautiful experience, a dance between external information and inner knowing.

My journey has been one of increasing awareness of both my outer and inner worlds, becoming more present and remembering what truly matters to me. I have learned that the dualistic perspective that separates inner and outer, personal time and work, stillness and action, fades as we feel more connected inside. When aligned with my values and intention to be of service, I experience a deep sense of peace in action. Each journey is unique, yet we are all interconnected. The story of how each of us can be a force for good continues to be written. My intention in writing this book is to offer a guide that helps us do the inner work that is needed as we embark on the new type of leadership that this world is longing for.

PART ONE

The Lost Connection

CHAPTER 1

Our Inner and Outer Crises Are Connected

"The old model is broken. We need to create a new one."
Former UN Secretary-General Ban Ki-moon

Collective and personal crises are part of life. Depending on where you live, your parents, grandparents, and great-grandparents might have experienced political upheaval, economic hardship, war and violence, or social suppression or exclusion. Every generation, it seems, has its specific challenges to deal with. And yet, these times feel special. Our environmental, economic, social, and political crises are not isolated events but are deeply interconnected and interrelated, creating a complex web of challenges that affect nearly every aspect of our lives.

The unprecedented speed of technological advance, coupled with global ecological collapse and economic and social instability suggests that the transformations ahead are not merely incremental but paradigm-shifting. We are living in a time where our collective actions—or inactions—will shape the future of the planet and humanity itself. To navigate this meta-crisis, we must redefine our relationship with nature, each other, and even ourselves. It is only by addressing our outer and inner crises simultaneously that we will be able to create a more resilient, compassionate, and sustainable future.

Our Outer Crises

Climate change is no longer an abstract scientific notion in the distant future. It is happening, right now. Of course, there have always been episodes of extreme weather, but the frequency of extreme events is increasing, and science largely attributes this change in climate to the way we humans live on this planet.[1]

The summer of 2024 set a new record, just after the previous one was recorded as the hottest over the past 2000 years.[2] I was interviewing a film-maker about his latest expedition to the Antarctic and he told me that when they arrived, the ice was covered with hundreds of dead penguins. He attributed their deaths to the abnormally mild temperatures that turned snowfall into rain. It had been raining for days, and young chicks who have not yet developed their waterproof feathers and protective layer of blubber are especially vulnerable to freezing to death as their defenseless bodies get soaked. Droughts, wildfires, floods, and extreme temperature fluctuations now afflict the globe on an unprecedented scale—a cataclysm not seen since the age of the dinosaurs. You may have come across images of long-submerged boats resurfacing in Lake Mead, the largest water reservoir in the United States, as its levels plummet alarmingly. Elsewhere, entire villages are being forced to relocate, threatened by rising river levels and the looming danger of floods. For years, we have witnessed massive evacuations due to wildfires in Southern Europe and North America, and the world has watched as animals narrowly escaped devastating floods in Brazil or raging bushfires in Australia. At the North and South Poles shrinking ice fields threaten the survival of wildlife and drive up sea levels. No continent or country escapes the consequences of climate change.

Our current way of living is not only causing climate change. We are currently crossing several planetary boundaries, which are the thresholds at which humanity can continue to thrive without causing large-scale, irreversible disruptions to the environment.[3] Scientists believe that we are experiencing the world's sixth mass extinction, in which a high percentage of distinct species of plants and animals become extinct over a relatively short period. This is a natural phenomenon, but the current rate of extinction is estimated to be 1,000–10,000 times faster than the natural extinction rate without the impact of human activity. The last mass extinction took place on this planet an estimated 65 million years ago, when a meteorite hit the Earth and wiped out all dinosaurs.[4] At the current rate of extinction we are losing biodiversity rapidly, which is critical to sustaining the ecosystem of our highly interconnected web of life, essential for human life on this planet.

A man-made chain of events lies at the root of this massive loss of biodiversity. We continue to convert biodiversity-sustaining land into land for intensive monoculture, so that we can eat whatever we want whenever we want it. These unsustainable food production and consumption habits contribute to emissions of greenhouse gasses, which in turn fuel climate change. One-third of the food that is produced at such high environmental cost is not even being consumed by us and is thrown away while over 733 million people, equivalent to one in eleven people worldwide and one in five in Africa, are facing hunger.[5] This is both unsustainable and insane.

Another planetary boundary that we are crossing arises from waste created by humans that is geologically new and significantly impacts the functioning of our Earth system processes.[6] We call these kinds of waste *novel entities*. Think of chemical pollution and microplastics, which can persist for centuries without dissolving, unlike biodegradable natural materials. We dump huge amounts of plastic waste into our environment daily, including an estimated 33 billion pounds of plastic into the oceans every year, the equivalent of two garbage trucks every minute.[7] Microplastics have been found in human blood samples, in the placentas of pregnant women, and in babies' poo[8]. This has consequences for human health and adds further pressure on biodiversity as animals die, tangled up in our waste or having ingested plastic, mistaking it for food. Once you pay attention, you see plastic everywhere.

The window for addressing the climate crisis is closing rapidly. The decade from 2020 to 2030 is critical for the survival of all species on Earth, yet we are falling far behind in tackling this challenge, with divisions growing deeper. Environmental tipping points now intersect with significant social and economic upheavals. After a historic two-year lockdown due to the COVID-19 pandemic, and following decades of peace, Europe is embroiled in the war in Ukraine. Meanwhile, the Hamas attack on Israel on October 7th, 2023, and the ensuing retaliation in Gaza have sent shockwaves around the world, stirring profound feelings of sorrow and anger. Ongoing conflicts in North Africa and other regions add to the global turmoil.

On the economic front, wealth is increasingly concentrated among the top 1%, while the erosion of the middle class in the US and elsewhere fuels widespread discontent. Long-standing systems and structures are being challenged, as seen in the growing awareness—and the resulting social tensions—surrounding the inclusion and equal rights of women, people of color, and the LGBTQ+ community. Simultaneously, rapid advances in artificial intelligence are set to dramatically reshape how we live and work. For many, this technological revolution only amplifies a sense of uncertainty in an already volatile world.

A Crisis of Being

Now, please take a couple of deep breaths with me. How did reading the above make you feel? Perhaps you did not feel much: you know we are in crisis and think there is nothing you can do about it; perhaps you feel worried and would like to make a difference, but you don't know how; or maybe you are already doing something, but you feel frustrated because it seems to be not enough? Whatever it is, if you feel stressed while reading this, that is completely normal. It is your nervous system responding to a perceived threat and activating your fight, flight, or freeze response.

We are in a dangerous situation and we all need to fight for this beautiful planet. By taking action, we regain a sense of agency and purpose. We all can and must play our part in caring for the wellbeing of our planet, for ourselves, our children, and the generations to come. However, if we don't want to create the same problems in a new disguise, we need to act from a place of connection rather than disconnection—within ourselves, with each other, and with nature.

That means, as individuals, we must do the inner work that helps us move from fear to love, recognizing that we are collectively facing not only an external meta-crisis but also an internal crisis of being.

Among executives and business leaders, chronic stress and burnout are all too common. Before the pandemic, burnout through overwork alone was estimated to be responsible for the deaths of 2.8 million people a year.[9] If you are not affected personally, you probably know friends or colleagues who had a burnout or were close to having one. In her research, *Harvard Business Review* journalist Jennifer Moss identifies our workload as the number one cause of stress and burnout, but other factors, such as a perceived lack of control, lack of recognition, poor relationships, lack of fairness, and a mismatch between our own values and those of the organization are also important contributors. The root cause is often organizational and cannot be fixed with well-intentioned wellness programs, such as yoga and meditation classes, alone. In her research, economist Noreena Hertz finds that employees around the world feel more disconnected from their work, and overall trust in others is substantially lower than in the 1980s.[10] She attributes this to technology and our modern ways of living, where increasingly atomization has made us feel more disconnected from each other. We can see this lack of trust also in increasing political and social polarization across the world.

The stress, anxiety, and loneliness that many are experiencing is not merely a personal issue; it is a symptom of a larger existential crisis facing humanity. A report on the mental state of the world in 2023, based on 400,000 responses from over 71 countries, highlights a significant decline in mental wellbeing that occurred between 2019 and 2020, persisted throughout the COVID-19 pandemic, and shows no signs of recovery across all age groups.[11] Interestingly, the data reveals a negative correlation between per capita GDP and average mental wellbeing. Initial investigations suggest early smartphone use, the consumption of ultra-processed foods, and weakened family bonds as major contributing factors.

The World Health Organization reports that, globally, one in seven adolescents, between 10 and 19 years old, experiences mental disorders, with anxiety disorders that may involve panic or excessive worry being the most prevalent in this age group.[12] In a survey by the University of Bath in the UK that interviewed 10,000 people between the ages of 16 and 26 years across 10 countries, 75% responded that they found the future frightening, and more than 50% said they felt sad, anxious, powerless, helpless, and guilty about climate change.[13] However, it is not just the awareness of our current environmental and social challenges that causes the younger generations stress, but, as the social psychologist Jonathan Haidt finds: "the ways that young people are responding, with activism carried out mostly in the virtual world, seem to be affecting them very differently compared to previous generations, whose activism was carried mostly in the real world."[14]

While there is certainly higher awareness and more data on these phenomena than several decades ago, there is some evidence that mental health issues have indeed been rising over the past decades. The fact remains that people are facing an inner crisis: feeling stressed, anxious, depressed, and lonely.

At first sight, this inner crisis may be surprising. Looking at the statistics, we humans have never had it as good as now: in general, we are materially better off, have more human rights, live longer, are more educated, and are less likely to become victims of violence.[15] And yet, many of us feel something's missing. Somewhere along the way, we have lost our connection to what matters. We have created an ever bigger and faster-spinning economic system, which made many people better off on the outside but led to increased stress on the inside. As a result, we experience an increasing disconnection from ourselves, each other, and nature.

Some researchers argue that, about ten thousand years ago, our ancestors were living mostly in harmony with nature and each other, in egalitarian communities characterized by a deep reverence for all life and a sense of unity with the greater whole.[16] On the other hand, there is plenty of evidence that we humans have always been one of the deadliest species in history.[17] Both perspectives can be true. The development of agriculture and, later, the Industrial Revolution, along with its division of labor, have brought an increasing sense of separation from nature as we were, quite simply, physically more and more detached from it. For example, when you buy your food or clothes, you typically have no idea where all the ingredients were grown or who made them. Despite these trends, there are still indigenous communities today that strive to maintain a close and sustainable relationship with their environment.

Our current economic system both drives and is sustained by this sense of separation. It is based on the economic theory that self-serving individualism and competition will lead to the expansion of overall social welfare through the invisible hand of the market. It relies on a mechanistic and linear interpretation of how our economy works, where markets tend toward equilibrium and crises are the result of external shocks to the system rather than inherent to the system. For example, nature, which is the basis of our economic interactions, is treated as external to the economic system. Environmental pollution is seen as an externality, an indirect cost to society due to market failure rather than our collective failure as market participants to produce, sell and buy products that do not harm the environment. This is not a very accurate description of how our economy works and ignores its complex nature.

There is ample empirical evidence that we humans are not just self-maximizing, competitive individualists but that we often do act altruistically.[18] Humanity has not survived by being the fittest in terms of strength or domination but through our ability to adapt and cooperate on a very large scale.[19] As humans, we need a new story of who we are and how we want to relate to this planet. It matters whether we simplify our understanding of human interaction in terms of selfishness or kindness, competition or cooperation, a sense of separation or interbeing.

The Nobel laureate Elinor Ostrom, who dedicated her life's work to studying problems of the commons, concludes that rather than trying to force people to behave ethically, "a core goal of public policy should be to facilitate the development of institutions that bring out the best in humans" to help the innovativeness, learning, adapting, trustworthiness, and cooperation of people.[20] We need to lead our organizations in a way that helps us remind each other of our inherent goodness and jointly create the change the world needs.

CHAPTER 2

Emerging New Leadership Skills

"We cannot solve our problems with the same thinking we used when we created them."
Albert Einstein

Our current economic system and the way we create growth is rapidly depleting the world's resources, warming the planet, and destroying functional ecosystems that are so necessary for our wellbeing and, ultimately, survival. We tend to talk about saving the planet but in all likelihood the planet will do just fine. It existed hundreds of millions of years before the arrival of humans, and it is likely to flourish without us, as evidenced by many examples of nature's recovery once left on its own. This decade is not about saving the planet but about redefining what it means to be human and our relationship with nature and each other.

The challenge business leaders and changemakers face today is that we are part of, and influenced by, the old systems we are trying to change. For example, in my conversation with Silvia, a senior manager at an international furniture and household goods manufacturer, she told me that over the last decade she had started to be more environmentally conscious and successfully implemented several sustainability projects within the company. However, she felt frustrated and questioned the meaningfulness and value of her initiatives as they just seemed too insignificant. "You know," she said, "I increasingly think there is something wrong with our system."

Many times, you will feel that your efforts are not enough or that you are fighting forces outside your control. Another example is Matthias, CEO of a large consumer goods company, who complained about feeling stuck in a rat race. When I suggested developing an inner practice to help him slow down, he said, "I can't. If I start to slow down, I will drop the balls and everything will collapse. Personally, physically and mentally, I don't need a break. I need a whole reset, which will take me months, at least."

I know Matthias is not alone in feeling this way. On our journey of creating change for the wellbeing of this planet, which also must include our own wellbeing, we may be confronted with contradictory choices: changing the system from our current position or changing what we are doing completely.

Whatever your decision may be, none of us alone will change the system, and yet each individual action matters. Because everything is interconnected, each one of us can be a piece of the puzzle in the change we want to see. As business leaders, we are often in a position to influence change on a broader scale. We do not have to wait for the rules of the system to change. Instead, we can rise to the challenge and recognize our ability and responsibility to co-create organizations and projects in service of nature and people to the best of our ability.

Navigating Complexity

We are used to thinking of our world in a reductionist way, that is to say with a mechanistic and linear view of how nature, organizations, and even our own bodies function. To understand a given system, we break it up into its parts and study how they work, just like the different pieces of a machine. However, as mentioned previously, this ignores the complex nature of most of our social and environmental systems. Complex systems are more than the sum of their parts and they develop emerging properties through the interaction of their parts. These emerging properties are new and not visible simply by observing the individual parts themselves.

When even one variable in a complex system deteriorates over time, the system eventually reaches a tipping point, where its behavior shifts irreversibly, often unexpectedly and rapidly, from one state into another. These tipping points are observable in nature, financial markets, and social movements. For example, the gradual deterioration of women's rights in Iran or the ongoing racial injustices in the United States created the conditions for a single event, such as the death of Mahsa Amini in Iran, or George Floyd in the USA, to spark mass protests. Similarly, the deterioration of the local US subprime housing markets triggered a global market collapse, leading to the Global Financial Crisis of 2008.

A complex systems view has three important insights for leaders who want to create positive change in the world.

First, to change the system we must begin by changing how we interact. This is not trivial because how we react to the outside world is often not conscious. We are shaped by our experiences, upbringing, habits, and culture, which are also influenced by the nature of a system itself. Our actions are determined by our thoughts and emotions, which most of the time we are not even aware of. Therefore, as leaders of change, we first need to train ourselves to be present and aware of our thinking and patterns. We need to expand our capacity to be with uncomfortable sensations, such as uncertainty or conflicting views, to then be able to move from an automatic reaction to a conscious response.

Second, when a system has become inherently unstable and is close to a tipping point, even a small event can lead to a massive change and reorganization of the whole system. Whenever you feel your action is just a drop in the ocean, remember that it only takes one additional drop to make a barrel full of water overflow. Your actions and your inner state of being influence others and can trigger wider movements of change.

Third, although our individual action matters, the system develops its own characteristics that are not foreseeable by just observing the individual parts themselves. This means that there can be, and often are, unintended consequences despite our good intentions, which makes fixing the system a lot more difficult. While we must reflect on the purpose of a given system and the intention of our behavior, it is not always the case that our action leads to the desired outcome.

Consequently, we need leaders who are humble, who genuinely care for the wellbeing of this planet, and who are confident enough to let go of their illusion of control. We need leaders who cultivate an open mind and heart, who are ready to collaborate, and who care more about getting it right than being right.

As our inner and outer crises continue to approach and cross social and environmental tipping points, old structures are collapsing, and these transitions bring a heightened element of uncertainty and disruption. They also bring a tremendous opportunity to reconnect within, start healing ourselves and our relationships, and co-create new systems that allow us to live in greater harmony with each other. As the UN Human Development Report in 2020 concluded:

> *"A new normal is coming, one that is more than uncertain; it is unknown. …Nothing short of a whole shift in mindsets, translated into reality by policy, is needed to navigate the brave new world of the Anthropocene, to ensure that all people flourish while easing planetary pressures."*[21]

New Leadership Skills

Today's leaders must be able to thrive in uncertainty, hold contradictory points of view, have a learning mindset, and be firmly rooted in a sense of purpose that is aligned with the wellbeing of our inner and outer environment. In the traditional business school, we were taught how to control our organizations, outsmart competitors, and set the right incentives to maximize the bottom line, whilst including the different stakeholders in the process to different degrees. These skills are helpful in a rather mechanistic, linear, and transaction-based view of the world. However, we now need skills that help us navigate into the unknown and co-create ways of living and working within a highly interconnected complex system.

New leadership styles are emerging. For example, Regenerative Leadership relies on this dynamic and emergent ecosystem view, where "regenerative business transforms our role and purpose from a what's-in-it-for-me approach to a mindset of collaboration, co-creativity, and contribution."[22] Regeneration refers to both the regeneration of life on Earth and a wider movement that asks leaders to be "moving out of our comfort zones to find a depth of courage we may have never known. It doesn't mean being right in a way that makes others wrong; it means listening intently and respectfully, stitching together the broken strands that separate us from life and each other. It doesn't mean hope or despair; it calls for action that is courageous and fearless. ...The ultimate power to change the world does not reside in technologies. It relies on reverence, respect, and compassion—for ourselves, all people, all life."[23]

Another example is the work of MIT lecturer Otto Scharmer, who sees our current crises as an 'Age of Disruption', the end of our old extractive, materially driven, 'Bigger is Better', me-oriented system, and an emerging future that requires us to shift the inner place from which we operate. It is a shift from an ego-system awareness to an eco-system awareness, which includes the wellbeing of all. He and his team teach an awareness-based sensing method to let go of old patterns of thinking and invite the emergence of new perspectives and actions. In this state, called Presencing, "listening originates outside the world of our preconceived notions. We feel as if we are connected to and operating from a widening surrounding sphere. As the presence of the heightened state deepens, time seems to slow down, space seems to open up, and the experience of the self morphs from a single point (ego) into a heightened presence and stronger connection to the sphere (eco)."[24] This method is similar to the meditation practice of resting in open awareness, which you will learn in Week Five and which, in my experience, is a state of emptiness or openness from which new thinking can emerge.

Ultimately, and most importantly, these emerging new leadership styles are a journey back to our hearts. This does not mean that we discard useful tools like rationality, linear problem solving, or goal orientation but that we acknowledge their limitations and reconnect to a deeper knowing within ourselves that is guided by our concern for the wellbeing of all life forms. It is a journey of integration and bringing back into balance where we have come out of balance: between humans and nature, the feminine and the masculine, individualism and community, competition and collaboration, productivity and rest. Ultimately, this is a continuous journey of healing, described by the poet and teacher Stephen Levine: "[To heal is] to touch with love that which we previously touched with fear." This definition of healing resonates deeply with my own experience. It is a process and commitment to act from a place of love rather than fear. Our role as leaders of change resembles a dance between our inner and outer awareness and our responsibility for the individual, the collective, and ourselves.

What is so exciting is that a wider movement of leading change from a place of presence and with a concern for our environment seems to be emerging. For example, Sharmer's course grew from 75 students to 75,000 students from 185 countries when it was made available as a Massive Open Online Course in 2015. Moreover, top-tier universities increasingly offer skills-based and topic-specific courses to prepare students to become values-driven leaders. Examples include the MindfulNYU initiative of New York University, Stanford Earth of Stanford University, the Social Enterprise initiative of Harvard University, The Environmental Change Institute of the University of Oxford, the Cambridge Institute for Sustainability Leadership of the University of Cambridge, the Transformational Leader Program at IMD Business School, or the Thrive: Lead with the World in Mind program by the THNK School of Creative Leadership, to name a few.[25]

The inner component of leadership, the quality of our presence, and a sense of connection to the greater whole are becoming increasingly important because our inner crisis of being and our outer crises are connected. If our task is nothing less than redefining what it means to be human and our relationship with nature and each other, we need a different way of thinking, being, and leading from which an entirely new system will emerge. This work is a highly rewarding but not necessarily comfortable journey. In this process, we must acknowledge what we don't know, where we may feel stuck, both collectively and in our own thinking, and continuously create an openness in our hearts and minds from which new insights and action can emerge. It is a continuous process of inner and outer work where our own healing facilitates the healing of the planet and vice versa.

Leadership skills for conscious impact

This book is designed to help you cultivate the skills needed to support you on your journey of creating meaningful change. Each week you will focus on one of six core leadership skills to help you navigate our current crises and to join an emerging new leadership that is creating positive change from a greater sense of connection with themselves, with others, and with nature.

The first week strengthens your ability to *cultivate presence and awareness*, which is the foundation and ongoing practice for leading change from within. Week Two focuses on *sensing our interbeing* to help experience yourself as part of the greater whole and see the connection between your practice and the world around you. Week Three focuses on *cultivating an open mind*, which is the necessary precondition for new thinking and ways of interacting to emerge. Week Four strengthens your capacity to be *comfortable with discomfort*, to help you move from automatic reaction and choose a conscious response amid increasing division and uncertainty. Week Five focuses on *cultivating an open heart* through wholesome states of being, helping you create change from a place of love and joy. Finally, in Week Six, you deepen your ability to *lead with purpose* by doing what creates meaning for you, being of service to the greater whole, and being clear about the values that matter to you on your journey of creating positive impact now.

Before we start, let me tell you what we know so far from neuroscience about the impact of mindfulness meditation on your body, mind, and heart. Over the last 10 years, the number of studies and publications that look at the effects of meditation has increased substantially. At some point, mindfulness got so popular that it seemed to be a cure-all derived from a watered-down version of an ancient practice full of wisdom. There are literally thousands of publications out there, now. Not all of the studies meet today's top scientific standards: they don't always distinguish between different types of meditation, and they use varying definitions of mindfulness. Despite recent advances in neuroscience, there is still a lot that serious researchers say they don't know (for a starter, we don't even know what *consciousness* really is). But there is also a lot we have learned so far, which I want to share with you.

Six core leadership skills to create conscious impact

Having practiced meditation for over twenty years, finding proof that what I was experiencing was real and not just something in my imagination was terribly exciting. Although my journey currently teaches me to attach less importance to my rational mind (often associated with the left side of the brain) and to trust and love my intuitive mind (associated with the right side of the brain), there is still this slightly nerdy side of me that loves facts. If this is also of interest to you, then let me summarize it for you here.[26, 27]

- **Focus**: Meditation sharpens your attention even after short periods of practice. Longer-term and intense periods of practice show longer-lasting effects of sustained concentration and increased vigilance.

- **Bias**: Studies show that mindfulness meditation can, after just a short time, reduce unconscious social biases. It also reduces the mind's negativity bias.
- **Compassion**: Loving-kindness and compassion meditation generally increase participants' willingness to act and reduce suffering while also activating the brain circuits connected to good feelings and love.
- **Resilience**: Meditation reduces stress reactivity of the brain after just a few hours of practice and improves with daily practice. Longer-term practice significantly increases the brain's ability to recover from stressful situations and a lasting shift in the baseline reactivity can be found in highly seasoned practitioners.
- **Mental health**: While meditation has been shown to reduce anxiety and depression, the effects seem to be small to moderate on their own and most helpful in conjunction with other interventions. Meditation may not be suitable for people with severe traumas and should be practiced with caution and guidance to help process the released emotions.

The research shows that what we focus on grows; the type of meditation you practice will determine the outcome it produces. One reason that mindfulness studies are not always comparable is that there is not one way to meditate, even within the mindfulness tradition. Specific meditations help us focus on:

- retaining our concentration and awareness
- investigating and understanding our mind
- connecting us with the qualities of our hearts.

I have sequenced the book to include all three types, first stabilizing focus and expanding our awareness, then investigating and working with the mind, and finally deepening our qualitative presence with compassion, loving-kindness, and joy. I decided to separate our practice into working with the body, mind, and heart to give a structure that makes it easy to learn. In practice, you will notice that everything is connected. The idea is to give your mindfulness practice a solid foundation. After a while, you may want to incorporate all these aspects into one sitting or decide to specifically focus on one of these areas, depending on your needs. For now, I invite you to follow the flow of the book and enjoy the insights of each practice.

A note before you begin

If you just read the book without the exercises or meditation, I hope you get some joy and inspiration from it. My deepest wish is that this book will help you to do some transformational work. I invite you to take the time to reflect and try the different practices to reconnect with your inner wisdom and discover how these practices can support you on your journey. If you want to take it slow and spend more than six weeks, let's say you want to spend two weeks on one chapter, this will also work well as long as you continue with the meditation practice and exercises. Six weeks is, in my experience, the time it takes for most people, especially if you are just starting your meditation practice, to start feeling the benefits and having aha-moments. So, you *do need* to make a commitment. Try to meditate five days a week or more. The guided meditations are short, 12-25 minutes, so that you can fit them into your schedule. If you find yourself off track, either with your practice or reading, simply start where you left off. If you want to go back, then go back. I will always guide you, but I will also encourage you to find your way and see what works for you. I am super excited to start walking on this journey together.

PART TWO

Reconnecting with Body, Mind, and Heart

RECONNECTING ON THE LEVEL OF THE BODY

Reconnecting on the level of the body is the first step in staying grounded and open, no matter what life throws at us. While our mind could be anywhere, our body is always in the now. Through connecting with the sensations in our body we learn to become more present and aware of both our inner and outer environments. Our body serves as an anchor from which we can reconnect within ourselves and expand our awareness to include others and the larger system we are part of and want to change. This connection is the basis for sensing our interbeing with all of life and for doing the inner work that allows us to create change from a sense of interbeing rather than separation.

Chapter 8
Leading with Purpose
Chapter 3
Cultivating Presence & Awareness
Chapter 4
Sensing our Interbeing
Chapter 5
Cultivating an Open Mind
Chapter 6
Being Comfortable with Discomfort
Chapter 7
Cultivating an Open Heart
LEADERSHIP SKILLS
FOR CONSCIOUS IMPACT

CHAPTER 3

WEEK 1 | CULTIVATING PRESENCE AND AWARENESS

"Between stimulus and response, there is a space. In that space is our power to choose our response. In our response lies our growth and freedom."
Victor Frankl

Slowing down in this fast world seems impossible. There are meetings to be held, reports to be written, investments to be made, funding to be raised, and ideally all this while saving the world from hunger, climate change, mass extinction, and social injustice. Right, I'm with you. Let's start by taking a breath.

Slowing down is not nice to have, it is a necessity. The faster you move, the harder it is to stay present and be aware. You can test this for yourself. Think of the last time you got up from your desk to get coffee, tea, or whatever you like to drink. Do you remember what else was happening, what sounds were present, how it felt to touch the cup, the taste of the first sip, and the second sip? How was your breath: deep or shallow? Were there any emotions present? If you like, next time you get a drink, do it extra slow and notice your present-moment experience through the sensations in your body. Perhaps you will find that this mundane experience suddenly becomes much more colorful and alive. When I slow down, breathe more deeply, and become aware of my inner and outer experiences, there usually arises a sense of joy or satisfaction from simply being.

When we rush things we miss things, and it is much harder to be aware of our inner experiences. Slowing down before a meeting can also be a powerful practice. When we rush from one meeting to the next, we can miss the opportunity to fully connect with our collaborators, listen deeply, think clearly, and be guided by a sense of purpose and service. Taking a few moments to connect with the sensations in our body, noticing if there is fear, judgment, or anger, and allowing ourselves to be with it, breathe and let go of the tension in our body, creates a sense of spaciousness in our mind and heart through which we can lead consciously, from a place of connection. We need to slow down to feel the sensations in our body, to notice the thoughts and emotions that are influencing us. When we get triggered in a conversation, our automatic reaction is a fight or flight response, which often is not what we would have wanted if we had felt we had a choice. Slowing down enough to notice when you are triggered and pausing for a split second gives you the space and freedom to respond differently.

Slowing down allows us to step aside from our human doing and remember our human being. Becoming aware of the sensations in our body can unfold a beautiful remembering of what it actually feels like to be human. It can reconnect us with a sense of wonder and appreciation of this precious human body through which we get to experience life: a body that is inherently self-regulating and even self-healing. As long as our body functions smoothly, we take for granted that it replaces about 330 billion cells every day and that it automatically heals itself when we cut our finger—isn't it amazing?

We tell ourselves that we can't slow down because we cannot afford to drop the ball at work, that we don't have time because things will fall apart without us or because we are afraid of missing out on important opportunities. In our current economic and social system, where we are told that time is money and faster is better, deliberately slowing down is a radical act. Sometimes, just slowing down a little, taking a break, and breathing deeply can feel like an act of revolution.

We tend to identify so much with our doing and measure our worthiness in terms of productivity. On the trading floor, my colleagues and I would take pride in a work-hard play-hard mentality, and compete on being able to function with as little sleep as possible.

Luckily, this attitude and culture has changed in many places. But our obsession with productivity is symptomatic of an economic system based on continuous growth and extraction of our natural resources.

I noticed that when I get sick, often my initial response is one of judgment and annoyance. Whenever I encounter resistance to slowing down, I find it useful to be with this resistance and ask myself, "What am I believing?" and "Is it true?" The answer is usually a fear-based belief and an overidentification with my separate sense of self. This separate self, sometimes also called *small self*, is overly attached to my thoughts and emotions, thinking that they define who I am. It keeps me from experiencing myself as part of the greater whole. For example, when I come down with a cold and have to change plans, I notice a voice in my mind saying, "You are letting people down" or "You are not doing enough." These thoughts trigger feelings of guilt and inadequacy, as if my value depended on my ability to perform and meet (often self-imposed) expectations. However, by sitting with these feelings and thoughts I begin to see how they are a construct of the small self. This helps me to stop clinging to immediate outcomes and solutions and, instead, surrender to life's flow which naturally includes slowing down to rest. Sometimes, it takes trust and courage to confront our fear of missing out, being irrelevant, not feeling useful, or simply feeling bored.

Slowing down is a commitment to being able to lead consciously. It is a commitment to working with nature rather than against it. Sometimes we need to slow down because our bodies are tired and we need rest. Other times, we need to slow down because we get so lost in our doing that we forget why we are so busy in the first place and what is truly important to us. In order to lead with intention and for our own wellbeing, these times call for a new balance between doing and being, resting and creating, stillness and action. The meaning and possibility of this may vary at different stages in our lives, but this much is clear: we need to slow down to reflect on what matters, to regenerate our bodies and minds, and to create the stillness from which wisdom can emerge. Nonaction is not the same thing as passivity or inertia; it's a dynamic and creative state of openness.[28]

Entering the Present Moment

In these times of distraction and uncertainty, being fully present is a superpower. Presence forms the basis for moving from automatic reaction to conscious response and thus for living your life in alignment with who you want to be. If we want to create positive change, we must be able to notice whether we are present and if our action aligns with our values. We must unlearn the habits and beliefs that no longer serve us and learn to lead with authenticity and courage. These changes come from acute self-awareness. Hence, learning to rest our attention in the present moment and cultivating an awareness of events and actions within and around us is the first core leadership skill for anyone who wants to create positive change.

Awareness refers both to your ability to direct your attention as well as to the entity which is perceiving, generally referred to as 'consciousness'. Think of it as using a flashlight to illuminate the thing you are focused on, leaving everything else in the dark. Awareness refers to the ability to shine a light as well as to the flashlight that is shining the light. As you focus on the different sensations in your body, you might notice that you can direct your awareness like a zoom lens into a specific part of your body, sensing how that part feels. Once you feel anchored in one part of your body, you also have the ability to broaden your awareness to include your whole body, noticing various sensations as they come and go. When your awareness is wide open, you can rest in awareness itself, sometimes referred to as *resting in open awareness*. There is no more zooming in; instead, every sensation that enters your awareness is consciously experienced.

Mindfulness is the practice of deliberately noticing our present-moment experience with a sense of curiosity and openness. We don't meditate to become great meditators (if there was such a thing), we meditate to help us stay open and centered amid all the busyness, uncertainty, and crises around us. Mindfulness meditation strengthens our ability to stay in a state of awareness outside of the meditation practice while we are busy with life.

Your body is your gateway to the present moment. Just because your body is in the right place—the board meeting, running errands, or having dinner with friends—does not mean that you are present. A quick way to know if you are truly present or not is to check if your body and mind are in the same place at the same time.[29] It may sound simple enough to do and yet, once you pay attention, you will notice how often your body is in one place and your mind in another.

Even with my daily meditation practice, I get lost. We all do. There are moments when I find my body at home sitting by the kitchen table and my mind is at work. I can see my daughter's excitement as she smiles at me and tells me something of great importance to her at that moment, but everything is in a haze because I am busy crafting an email in my head. When I notice and finally pay attention, the moment of connection has passed. I ask her to repeat what she just said, but she is already off to new endeavors, playing with her brother, completely absorbed in the game. Noticing a small sting in my heart, I remember that the gift of life only unfolds in the present moment and that everything is temporary.

"Isn't it strange how we always think we have to be somewhere else?" said my teacher Tara Brach during the opening seminar of my teacher training in Washington, DC. At that moment, I felt so seen in my constant urge to be in the future or dwell in the past. Usually, I am planning something or judging how I handled a situation in the past, analyzing how I could do better next time. And apparently it is not just me: most of us do this all the time and we don't even notice it. Perhaps it would even be funny if our time on this earth was not so precious. With our minds constantly stuck in memories of the past or imaginations of the future, we are missing our life, which can only reveal itself in the present moment. This robs us of the opportunity to lead our lives consciously, courageously, and with joy.

Ultimately, whether you want to deliver an inspiring speech in front of an audience, close an important deal, or spend quality time with your family and friends, your ability to stay in the present moment is the key to creating a positive impact and sensing what truly matters in any given moment.

However, it is not easy to be present these days. For many of us, our outside environment has become so busy, fast-paced, and noisy that we feel continually stressed. We live in a time of continual stimulation. We feel an obligation to be available anywhere, anytime, across multiple channels and devices. We also have access to information anywhere, anytime, across multiple channels and devices, and the state of Always On leaves our mind and body in constant alert. In the short term, we adapt but in the long term this hyper-alert state becomes addictive, making us want to check our emails, messages, and social media feeds even more. We check our phones every few minutes adding up to hundreds of times a day, often right after waking up or before going to sleep.

Being constantly switched-on has fragmented our experience of time and left our minds scattered, overwhelmed, and unfocused.[30] However, it is not just technology that is to blame for our inability to concentrate: our food and lifestyle also matter. Our increasing difficulty in focusing is, arguably, a symptom of these fast-paced, industrialized, consumption-driven times.[31] Eventually, our bodies reach a state of simultaneous overstimulation and numbness. We are over-entertained and under-joyed and have lost our ability to focus on what matters.

Our challenge is to find the right balance between being present in and part of this world while being wise enough to cultivate habits that serve our wellbeing. I believe this balance, and how to achieve it, can look different for different people, depending on where we live, and on our personality, culture, and stage in life. The good news is that the latest research shows that we have not lost our physical ability to focus[32] but that it takes a deliberate effort to cultivate it. Mindfulness meditation is a proven method to regain your attention and can help you find that balance. By becoming more and more present, we are better able to observe the feedback loops between our inner world and our behavior. Doing so with a sense of curiosity and kindness rather than judgment (*Oh, why can't I be more disciplined?*) creates the spaciousness that allows us to see the needs underlying an unhealthy habit and help us choose a healthy one instead.[33]

Awakening Your Senses

For me, the practice of mindfulness is one of becoming ever more alive. And our body serves as the gateway to the present moment through our senses. By bringing our attention to the sensations of seeing, hearing, tasting, smelling, and touching, our inner and outer worlds meet, and we experience life. Sensing our body grounds us in the present moment and brings our mind and body into the same place. Noticing our sensations and starting to feel our body from the inside out is an opportunity to feel more alive and regain a sense of awe for this life, similar to that of a young child. I love watching my children run, dance, and skip throughout the day, jumping into the coldest water, squeaking for joy, and being so excited when eating an ice cream. Although children are generally not very mindful, in the sense that they are not aware of being aware, they have this beautiful capacity to be in the present moment and explore life with all their senses.

You can reconnect with your senses and experience this sense of wonder anywhere, at any time. If you like, take a moment right now to notice where you are, look around and notice the shapes and colors in your environment, feel how your body touches the surface you are standing or resting on, notice the sounds around you, the taste in your mouth, any particular smell, or simply the sensation of the breath entering and leaving through your nose. Pause. No need to analyze or judge your experience—simply allow yourself to be with whatever is present for you. Breathe.

Even during this small exercise, you might have noticed that your mind likes to hijack your focus and that keeping your attention in one place can be quite challenging. Focusing on the breath is a helpful way to bring your attention to the body. When you notice your mind wandering, you can redirect your attention to your breath and use it as an anchor to collect your mind and bring awareness to the sensations inside your body.

If you feel some parts of your body better than others—that is normal. You might experience sensations like tingling, heat or cold, throbbing, itching, and also numbness. Don't judge yourself if you feel physically or emotionally numb. In our modern days, we are exposed to so many more stimuli than our ancestors. And each time our senses are activated, our nervous system processes this information and triggers a reaction. When we feel threatened, our Sympathetic

Nervous System gets activated and triggers a fight, flight, or freeze response. Being confronted with difficult emotions that we are not yet ready to process, either through the microtrauma of constant stress, or traumatic events in our child- and adulthood, we tend to seek relief by disassociating from our body through numbing or distractions. With mindfulness, we practice gently bringing awareness back to our inner experience of sensations, emotions, and feelings—noticing, sensing, and allowing. By reconnecting with our body, step by step, we return to life and awaken to the extraordinary experience of being human. Over time, this practice can create more flow and openness where there is numbness or contraction.

As you connect to the sensations and feelings in your body, you will notice that automatically your mind judges the experience as either pleasant, unpleasant, or neutral. I will explain how to actively work with emotions in Chapters Five and Six. For now, let's focus on how this feels in your body and how that influences your behavior. We tend to ignore the neutral sensations and instinctively try to maximize pleasant ones (*Oh, let's have another scoop of ice cream*) and try to avoid unpleasant sensations (*Oh, let's have that difficult conversation another time*).

With mindfulness and during meditation, you practice staying present with the pleasant and the unpleasant sensations in your body, neither clinging to the former nor avoiding the latter. This way, you are expanding your capacity to be with pleasure and with pain, which is crucial for our role as changemakers. We create the necessary inner space to see nature's beauty and its destruction, to see our inherent goodness and our capacity for violence. Life is full of tensions and contradictions. By practicing staying present without clinging or avoiding, we can find new freedom: to feel fully alive and respond to our present-moment experience from a deep sense of connection independent of the current internal or external 'weather'. This is the freedom to feel everything and react to nothing.

The Healing Power of Silence

Slowing down, let alone being in silence, was not on Laura's agenda. She did not have time for that. Being an award-winning entrepreneur and leader, passionate about sustainability, she had an organization to run as CEO and no time to lose in creating the most impact she could. Until one evening, playing with her 2-year-old daughter, she was stopped in her tracks. In a freak accident, she fell and sustained what doctors diagnosed as a minor traumatic brain injury. For her, there was nothing minor about it. Laura experienced intense pain and the noises of everyday life felt like they were piercing her brain, triggering bursts of anxiety attacks. Performing previously simple tasks like engaging in a conversation or making breakfast for her daughter would leave her exhausted and dizzy. For a doer like Laura, who wanted to engage with others and drive change while also being a good parent, this situation was a nightmare. She had a hard time accepting her current circumstances and struggled to find medical cures and doctors that would help her get better. It was only when no quick fix could be found that she began to see how she had been an advocate for environmental sustainability for years but had completely ignored her body's signals calling for her own sustainability and regeneration. Given the urgency of the global problems, self-care had seemed indulgent and unnecessary, but now she had no choice other than to surrender to her current situation.

Ultimately, spending time in nature and being in silence helped Laura get back on her feet. "The sun, nature, and meditation became my medicine and my cure, and slowly the internal despair, the frustration, and the sadness were replaced by a newfound peaceful way of being grounded in my own body. I felt stronger and more content and happier than ever."[34]

With our nervous systems being in constant overdrive, our bodies long for silence. Silence is healing. Silence is not the absence of sound, it is the absence of noise, which is an unwanted distraction through the stimulation of our senses. For example, it could be external noise, such as an overload of information or the constant exposure to internal noise, such as the continuous internal chatter in our mind. Silence is the experience of a deep sense of presence that people experience and describe in different ways and yet all of us know it in one way or another.[35] It is the presence of continuous noise that keeps us from feeling connected within ourselves and aligned with what matters to us.

I have found that integrating pockets of silence into my daily life is a powerful way to facilitate deep presence. One of the (many) great things about having a dog is that you have to go out for a walk, no matter what the weather and no matter how much is on your plate. Previously, I used that time to make calls and get things done for which I did not have to be at my desk. Back home, I noticed that although I had just spent an hour outside in nature, I did not feel refreshed. My body had made all the right moves, but my mind had been somewhere else. Now, I make it a habit to leave my phone at home. After an initial separation anxiety (*What if something urgent happens and I cannot be reached?!*) I am able to take my dogs for a walk in silence, practicing being present, taking in the beauty of nature, and staying the leader of my pack.

Scientific studies show that silence restores our nervous system, facilitates the growth of new brain cells responsible for learning and memory, and improves our ability to deal with complexity, something we all need more of.[36] When we reduce the noise around us, our nervous system can relax and signal to our body that we are safe, activating the Parasympathetic Nervous System which slows our heart rate, lowers our blood pressure, promotes digestion, and enables a state of relaxation that allows for regeneration.

Ultimately, the practice is learning to find silence amidst all the activities we do.[37] Through deep presence, we can reduce our inner noise and listen to the whispers of our hearts, reminding us of our true nature and what matters to us. It is in this silence that we can find answers and solutions to our problems beyond the analytical and habitual mind. And it is here that we can regain our sense of connection within ourselves, with each other, and with nature.

Everything is Temporary

As you become more present you may notice that everything is changing all the time. The sound that a moment ago pulled away your concentration is gone. The itch that you did not scratch disappeared by itself. As you become stiller and more present, you notice your breath coming and going, blood flowing, nerves pulsing, and your heart beating sometimes fast and sometimes slow. Life never stands still.

A teacher of mine once asked me to reflect on this impermanence and notice everything temporary and everything permanent in my life. When I opened the fridge, I noticed the yogurt, the jam, and the cheese... definitely impermanent! The bowl of fruit, also impermanent. I looked outside in the garden, the leaves on the trees, impermanent. What about the more solid stuff, the trees themselves, the ceramic bowl, sure it can last decades, perhaps centuries, but forever? When my dog came, looking at me with his deep brown eyes full of love, my heart contracted. He, too, was impermanent. This discovery went on for weeks and I couldn't wait to see my teacher again to tell her how depressing this exercise was. The only thing I could think of that seemed to last forever was the plastic pollution in our oceans, but even plastic breaks down over hundreds of years. Noticing the distress my little experiment was causing me, my husband laughed and said, "But our love, that lasts forever!"

Everything changes all the time. Even if our love were to last forever, it too would be different, because we will be different. Every moment is unique and every phenomenon is temporary. To stay present in the moment thus requires us to give up our resistance to change and come into resonance with life. We begin to stop clinging to the good (pleasant) and to stop avoiding the bad (unpleasant), staying deeply present and open as life unfolds.

This Precious Life

The problem is that we think we have time. In many ways, we treat our body the same way we treat our Earth: we deplete it and take it for granted as long as it is functioning. Only when it starts not to work anymore do we tend to wake up and listen to its signals of exhaustion. But just like this earth, our body is nothing short of a miracle!

For decades, we have seen that our current ways of living and creating economic growth would lead us to where we are now (heat waves, massive floods, species dying, people fleeing...) but we thought we, or our politicians, had time to fix it. The reality is that the environmental changes that scientists predicted decades ago are now happening faster than expected. When it comes to our own lives and the lives of the people we love most, the reality is that we do not know how much time anyone has. All we know is that our time here on Earth is limited. It was like that for our ancestors, and it is like this for all eight billion humans on this planet right now.

Our time here is precious, too precious not to be awake, not to be fully present and connected in this human body, too precious not to listen to the cries of our hearts that long for connection, meaning, and healing. And we can do this. Because our inner and outer crises are connected, this time, with all its uncertainty and suffering, presents an extraordinary opportunity for us humans to redefine what it means to be human, and how we treat each other, ourselves, and the living environment around us.

If, like me, you have enough to eat, you have a home with electricity, you've had an education, and you have the financial and legal freedom to, by and large, make your own decisions—then we have been extraordinarily lucky. This is not to negate all we have achieved through hard work and the suffering that has and will be taking place in our lives, but the bigger picture is that our precious life here has put us in the extraordinary position of being able to create a positive impact in our lives and in the lives of others. With this ability comes responsibility, and we all know this. It's just that we keep getting lost in our busyness, in our self-circulating thoughts, and thinking that we first need to be somewhere else to do what is important right now. We have the responsibility and the opportunity to live our lives fully, in a way that creates more connection than separation, to love our lives, and become the pieces of the puzzle of creating positive change.

Setting Up Your Meditation Practice

Developing a regular meditation practice will strengthen your ability to stay present and deepen your awareness. Although you can practice mindfulness throughout the day—remembering to pause and reconnect with the sensations in your body, using your breath to relax and collect your mind—your meditation practice is like going to the gym. Over time, meditation can literally rewire your brain.[38] During the next six weeks, we will train different muscles, which will help you to access the clarity (wisdom) and heartfulness (compassion) that will support you on your journey as a leader and changemaker. It is during this formal part of the practice that we can experience and remember our interbeing with the rest of the world perhaps most easily. A truth that is so easily forgotten, when we are busy writing emails, planning meetings, devising strategies and frantically working off our to-do-lists.

The following steps can help you to develop a practice that works for you:

- **Find a time**: Go through a typical day and see where you can most easily reserve 15-30 minutes for your practice. The meditations in the book are short, between 12-25 minutes[39] so that you can easily incorporate them into your day.

  For some, the best time to meditate may be getting up earlier and sitting before doing anything else. I love the idea but could never put it into practice consistently. The time that works for me is the moment my kids are out of the house and before I write my first emails or schedule any calls. Any time that works for you is the right time. However, my recommendation is to pick a time in the first half of the day so that you can bring those benefits into your day. You can then always do another short meditation in the evening if you want to. Consider making a distinction between your schedule during the week and at the weekend and plan accordingly.

- **Find a place**: You want a place that is fairly quiet, where you can be alone and where you feel safe. It helps to have a dedicated place for your practice. If you can, create a space at home with a meditation cushion and mat that is always there for you to see, to motivate and remind you of your commitment to the practice. I have this in my office, along with a flower, candle, and a little Buddha because it reminds me of beauty and wisdom and helps me to connect with my heart. However, none of this is essential. You can meditate perfectly well sitting on a chair and no accessories are needed. The point is to find a place that works for you and to make it as enjoyable as possible. Don't let your idea of a perfect way to practice stand in the way of practicing regularly. I had one student who found the ideal time and place to be in her car; another chose the bathroom. These were places where they would be undisturbed by their families.

- **Make a plan**: What else would help you to try this practice over the next six weeks? You may consider adjusting the frequency. Ideally, you want to practice every day but why not start with five days a week? I generally resist having to do something every day and easily resent it the moment I feel obliged. Having a few joker days can help to simply get going. After a while, meditation becomes like brushing your teeth. If you don't do it, you feel out of sorts and miss it. Make a plan ahead of time for what you'll do when you get sidetracked—life happens. Perhaps you want to redo the previous chapter/week to get back into your practice. The most important part is not to get discouraged and to get back on track. You've done harder things: you can do this.
- **Just do it**: During the meditation, I will guide you on what to do. You can access the meditation on your phone or device and simply follow my voice, or use the script provided in the appendix. Don't overthink this and don't expect to avoid having thoughts. As long as you are paying attention and notice when you get lost in your thoughts and then remember to come back, you are doing it right. If there are lots of thoughts, if there is restlessness, impatience, or doubt… then this is your practice. Let yourself feel whatever comes up for you and come back to your anchor of attention.
- **Enjoy**: We are much better able to learn something if we enjoy it. One day your meditation may feel cumbersome, then it may be helpful to bring in a sense of curiosity, perhaps even humor. Another day you may find it easy to connect with a sense of spaciousness or one of the heart qualities, then let yourself enjoy these moments. Soak them up, until they inevitably pass again. Relax and observe. Observe and relax.

Week 1–Going Deeper: Understanding Your Nervous System

Our nervous system is the foundation through which we experience life. It is a complex network of nerves and cells that enables communication between our brain, spinal cord, and all connections to our organs and body, and vice versa. This system can be primarily divided into two main components: the Central Nervous System and the Peripheral Nervous System.

The Central Nervous System encompasses the brain and spinal cord. The brain is the command center, processing and interpreting sensory information received through the spinal cord and issuing directives on how to respond. The spinal cord acts as a crucial information highway, facilitating the flow of sensory and motor signals and playing a key role in reflex actions.

The Peripheral Nervous System branches out from the Central Nervous System. It includes all the nerves extending to other parts of the body, including muscles, glands, and organs. It is further segmented into the Somatic Nervous System, which controls voluntary movements and sensory information transmission, and the Autonomic Nervous System. The Autonomic Nervous System operates subconsciously, regulating vital functions such as breathing, heartbeat, digestion, and stress response.

Within the Autonomic Nervous System, there are two critical subdivisions:

The Sympathetic Nervous System kicks into gear when you are under stress or in danger, enhancing alertness and energy by accelerating the heart rate and boosting hormone production, preparing the body for a fight, flight, or freeze response. This system is also active during positive stress scenarios, such as intense concentration or physical activity.

The Parasympathetic Nervous System promotes a 'rest and digest' state, active when you rest, helping the body to calm and recuperate after the stress has subsided by slowing the heart rate, enhancing digestion and metabolism, and regulating inflammation.

A well-regulated nervous system maintains balanced stress responses, allowing for swift recovery within our[40] optimal range between the Sympathetic and Parasympathetic Nervous Systems—our window of tolerance.[41] In contrast, a dysregulated nervous system can trap us in states of hyperarousal, characterized by excessive activation of the Sympathetic Nervous System or hypoarousal, which is associated with a shut-down of the Parasympathetic system. During the former, you may experience a persistent state of panic, anxiety, or rage, and physical symptoms such as a fast heart rate, shallow and quick breathing, muscle tension and high levels of cortisol and adrenaline. In contrast, the latter state is characterized by feelings of immobilization, brain fog, dissociation, depression, mental and physical fatigue with irregular heartbeats, shallow and irregular breathing, digestive issues and a sensitive immune system.

An overstimulated and dysregulated nervous system can have a significant effect on our leadership, and on our ability to make decisions and take the right actions. Recognizing the symptoms of when we are in hyper- or hypoarousal can help us better understand our window of tolerance and proactively engage in activities that restore balance.

Mindfulness, nourishing social interactions, spending time in nature, play and laughter can all contribute to restoring a healthy nervous system, as do nutrition, exercise, and sleep. Breathwork has a direct effect on the vagus nerve and is the only way in which we can directly influence our Autonomic Nervous System. Hence, it is particularly effective in managing acute anxiety, enhancing concentration, and improving overall emotional regulation.[42]

Week 1–Questions and Exercises

Below you will find the reflections and exercises for this week. The questions are intended to help you reflect on how presence and awareness affect your life and where you feel called to make changes. As mentioned earlier, our meditation practice is only a preparation for becoming more present and connected in our daily life and work. The exercises are ways in which you can integrate short moments of mindfulness to cultivate and experience being present and aware. My suggestion to you is to stay curious and playful. You don't have to do all the exercises or answer all the questions: experiment with it and notice what happens.

Questions

- How does not having my mind and body in the same place affect my work and relationships?
- What helps me to slow down and cultivate presence in my everyday life? (e.g. eating alone, putting your smartphone on flight or focus mode, regular walks in nature.)
- Where do I feel numbness in my life? What are the feelings that I am unwilling to feel in my role as a business leader and changemaker?
- What is my attitude toward my body? And how would I treat it differently if I could fall in love with my body in all the ways it makes this life possible?
- Reflecting on impermanence, what emotions are present and how could they serve me in my role as a leader and changemaker?

Exercises

- Pause several times a day and notice: "Where is my mind right now?" Notice the sensation of your breath and reconnect within your body, e.g. by feeling how your feet connect to the floor. Continue what you have been doing with full presence for as long as you can.

- Slow down to reconnect with your senses several times a day, e.g. when you wash your hands, feel the sensation of the water on your skin, and notice where your mind is. When you go for a walk, notice the air touching your skin, the different colors, sounds, and smells around you.
- Take a meal in silence. Slow down and appreciate a healthy and delicious meal, noticing its texture, colors, smell, and taste with a sense of curiosity. Take your time, explore the sensations in your mouth. Notice any urge to swallow or to chew fast, respond consciously. Reflect on this experience.
- In your next meeting, while someone else is speaking, notice where your mind is. Are you fully present to what is being said or already preparing a response or waiting for the next moment to present your point of view? What difference does it make if you are consciously present, listening with your whole body to what is being said?

Week 1–Daily Meditation

Meditation on the Body

This week's meditation is designed to cultivate being present and aware of the sensations in your body.

Details about accessing this meditation can be found on my website.

https://www.susannevonderbecke.com/consciousimpact/meditation1

A transcript of this meditation can be found in the appendix.

Week 1–Optional Breathwork

Alternate Nostril Breathing

This breathing practice, also known in yoga as Nadi Shodhana, calms the mind and enhances mental clarity and focus by balancing the left and right hemisphere of the brain. It can help you balance your nervous system when you feel anxious and stressed. This practice is best performed seated, with your spine straight and your shoulders and belly relaxed.

1. Place your left hand comfortably on your lap. Fold the index and middle fingers of your right hand toward your palm, leaving the thumb, ring and little fingers extended.
2. Close the right nostril by gently pushing your right thumb against the soft part just below the bones of your right nostril.
3. Inhale slowly through the left nostril, filling your lungs with air.
4. Close your left nostril by gently pressing your ring finger against the soft part underneath your left nostril. Now both nostrils are closed by the thumb and ring finger. Hold this for a second or two.

5. Release your right thumb and slowly exhale through your right nostril.
6. After the exhalation, pause and inhale through your right nostril while the ring finger continues to close the left nostril.
7. Close the right nostril with your thumb. Pause briefly, then release the ring finger from the left nostril and exhale through your left nostril.
8. Continue to alternate nostrils for 3–5 minutes and finish by exhaling through the left nostril.

Practice it as needed throughout the day or as a preparation for your meditation.

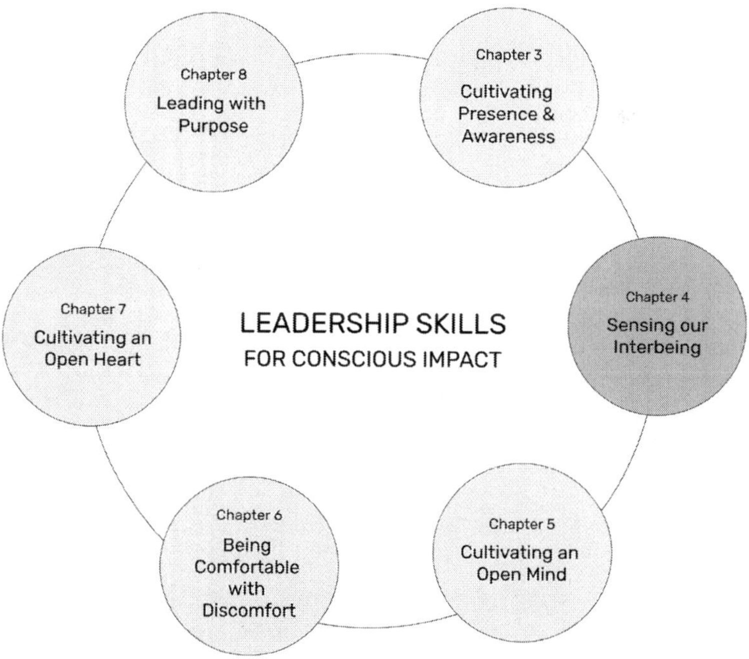
LEADERSHIP SKILLS
FOR CONSCIOUS IMPACT
Chapter 3
Cultivating Presence & Awareness
Chapter 4
Sensing our Interbeing
Chapter 5
Cultivating an Open Mind
Chapter 6
Being Comfortable with Discomfort
Chapter 7
Cultivating an Open Heart
Chapter 8
Leading with Purpose

CHAPTER 4

WEEK 2 | SENSING OUR INTERBEING

"You are not a drop in the ocean. You are the entire ocean in a drop."
Rumi

The common source of our inner and outer crises is our sense of separation from ourselves, each other, and nature. But when we take time to question who we really are we can sense that our perspective of what separates us from others is what Albert Einstein called "an optical delusion of consciousness"[43] where we experience ourselves as separate although we are part of the whole.

In physics, as we analyze matter in ever smaller parts we find that each big part is made of many small ones and the small ones are made of even smaller parts. Similarly, ecology reveals the complex interplay and mutual reliance among various species and their environment, ourselves included, which give rise to different ecosystems, which in turn are often interconnected with other ecosystems. In mindfulness, the understanding that nothing exists separately from anything else, is referred to as *interbeing*.[44] It is the recognition that we cannot exist by ourselves and that we exist because of those who came before us, that we exist because of an incomprehensibly complex web of life, including the sun, the earth, the water, the air, our parents, our ancestors and a myriad different life forms. This idea is also captured by the terms *interdependence* or *interconnection*, which are sometimes used interchangeably.

Remembering that we are part of a bigger whole, that we are not separate from nature nor from each other, is crucial for making the necessary shift to create change from a place of connection rather than separation. Our common understanding of what makes us successful business leaders is based on an individualistic, mechanistic, and extractive way of living that feeds into our illusion of separation. The result is not only the destruction of nature and rising social tensions but an increasing sense of loneliness, anxiety and lack of meaning.

Shifting the way we relate to the world around us starts within. It is not a matter of understanding our interdependence intellectually but allowing ourselves to sense and feel it. Reflecting on our interdependence not just as a human species but also in our own lives can leave us feeling both deeply grateful and deeply vulnerable.

The more connected we feel with nature and each other, the more connected we feel within ourselves. At the same time, the more connected we feel within ourselves, the more we are touched by the suffering around us and motivated by the wish to alleviate this suffering. Consequently, sensing our interbeing helps us to facilitate both our own healing and that of the planet. In that sense, that call to save our planet is a call to drop our illusion of separation and save ourselves by creating new ways of thinking and being that are in service of the wellbeing of the whole.

Before we explore this idea more concretely, I'd like to invite you to do a little experiment with me. When we are stuck in our perception of ourself as a solid, separate self, a helpful reflection to meditate on is: *who am I?* Take a moment right now and ask yourself, who is reading these words? Pause and sit with this question for a moment. Perhaps the answer that comes to you is: *well, me, of course!* And where is "me"? You might look at your body and think, this is me. But you are not your foot, or your leg, or your arm, or your head. You can look even further inside and see if you can find yourself or "me" in your organs, for example, your heart or your brain. Upon further contemplation, you will see that what you consider to be "me" is nowhere to be found and that who you really are is awareness itself.

Now, I've just thrown you into the deep end of mindfulness meditation, and perhaps you are feeling a little confused or even unsettled. I've noticed in my own practice and with students, beginners and experienced alike, the process of letting go of our *idea* of who we are—our body, our education, our profession, our wealth, all our stories of everything we did and all that has happened to us—can be frightening. Holding on to the idea of being a solid, separate self can initially give us a sense of security. Because who are we if not that? Are we nothing? No, we don't need to be afraid, we are everything. We are "the entire ocean in a drop," as Rumi said.

Interbeing with Nature

In the hustle of modern life, there is an increasing disconnection between human existence and the natural world. This detachment is not just physical, as more and more of us live in big cities and urban environments, but also psychological, as the recognition of human-nature interdependence fades. Yet, this understanding is crucial; acknowledging that we are inherently part of nature has profound implications for our wellbeing, our understanding of sustainability, and, ultimately, the future of humans and other species on this planet.

We are nature. Firstly, it is important to recognize that we are biological beings. Just like any other form of life on Earth, our existence is a direct manifestation of nature's processes. We are born of nature; our bodies grow, adapt, and function according to biological principles established by millions of years of evolution. For example, our very survival depends on breathing oxygen, a gas produced largely by phytoplankton and plants, which ties our existence fundamentally to the existence and health of the world's forests and oceans.

However, modern living often obscures these basic dependencies. Urbanization exemplifies this as we receive water from taps, food from grocery stores, and we're sheltered from climate realities by built environments. These conveniences are so integrated into our lifestyles that it's easy to forget they originate from nature. The water cycle, agriculture, and even the raw materials for constructing our shelters are all processes of, or products from, the Earth. We're not separate or elevated from the rest of the ecosystem; we're a deeply embedded component of it.

We are part of nature and nature is part of us. Our bodies are composed of the same fundamental elements as the natural world—

carbon, hydrogen, oxygen, and others. We are made of the same building blocks as trees, animals, and the Earth itself. Our human body includes non-human cells in the form of microorganisms like bacteria, fungi, and viruses that are vital to keep our body running healthily. Just like all living organisms, we go through life cycles of birth, growth, reproduction, and death. This mirrors the life cycles of plants and animals in nature.

I once attended a workshop on the female menstrual cycle and the presenter explained how it can be understood as phases of winter, spring, summer, and autumn. The premise was that the better we learn to accept our body's need for rest during winter, the more energy and flow we will experience afterward in spring and summer. The presenter suggested we get to know our cycles and that we respect our need for rest at the end of our cycle by already making more space in our calendars, taking on fewer responsibilities and meetings. I noticed two participants, a finance professional and a lawyer, getting quite agitated and upset. Firstly, the idea of our periods influencing our performance was so contentious because, since women have entered the same professional roles as men, we have tried to prove that we are just as capable and that our periods do not affect our performance. Secondly, it just seemed entirely impractical, even if we would be more productive when we allowed our bodies to rest. The reality is that resting is a regenerative process that is a prerequisite for high performance, for women and men alike. But in line with an economic system that requires continuous growth and where the mere signal of a decline in GDP growth leads to lower stock market valuations, we treat our bodies as vehicles for production that must go on, no matter what season we might be in.

As humans, we are all influenced by the cycles of life but instead of listening to their rhythm, we regard rest as a sign of weakness, lack of discipline and control. Our modern way of living does not leave much room to honor the natural cycles of birth and death, planting and harvesting, creativity and rest. When we look at nature, whether it is the trees, the tides of the sea, animal populations, or our bodies, life is a continuous flow of expansions and contractions. But since our economic model requires constant growth, it seems we have come to believe that life should be about expansion only. Our businesses must be growing all the time, our economies must be growing all the time, and just the threat of entering a recession is bad news. As individuals, we hardly allow ourselves to slow down, to hibernate, to reflect upon and process everything that is happening in our lives because we are so busy working, checking tasks off our to-do lists, and being productive. But we are not separate from nature and our wellbeing is intricately linked to our ability to process our continuous stimulation and experiences.

Our health is also tied to the health and balance of the ecosystems we are a part of. But instead of feeling part of nature and our ecosystem, we treat it as something external to us, something that should be dominated and controlled to feed, shelter, and entertain humanity. The idea of humans as separate from or above nature is a cultural construct that hasn't been universally adopted. Many indigenous cultures around the world have long recognized the importance of living in harmony with nature. They see themselves as part of the web of life, with a deep respect for all beings, often passed down through stories, rituals, and sustainable practices. This respect results in a more sustainable way of living, emphasizing that every action has consequences for the environment that, in turn, affect us.

Recognizing ourselves as part of nature can be profoundly healing and grounding. The concept of forest bathing from Japan or the push for more green spaces in urban environments stems from understanding the positive effects of nature on human mental health. Studies show that interacting with nature reduces stress, improves mood, and enhances cognitive functioning. It reminds us of our place within the larger ecosystem, fostering empathy and a sense of belonging.

A friend of mine who advises companies on implementing sustainability practices once told me that the idea of just implementing new metrics and reporting on the results is missing the point. "Sustainable is something you become," he said. I was skeptical because it did not sound very practical or efficient, but now I think I know what he meant. As long as we cannot sense our interconnection with nature, as long as our environment stays something out there rather than being something that is part of us and that we are part of, these metrics too easily become a tick-the-box exercise in the best case and greenwashing in the worst. Seeing ourselves as part of nature and overcoming our illusion of separation is integral to creating real change.

Interbeing with Others

Recognizing that we are part of nature, that our body is made of and sustained by plants, animals, and minerals reminds us of our interdependence. Honoring our interdependence does not come naturally in our individualistic, market-based society. Our economic system, based on competition for a finite amount of resources, naturally creates a sense of scarcity and separation. In this competition for resources, we are taught to be independent and primarily rely on our self-interest. Generally, we attribute our success to our hard work and perhaps an element of luck. Although we might recognize that we have had helpers along the way, who opened doors in our careers, educated us, built our homes, produced our food, raised and birthed us, most of us still attribute our success to our own brilliance and dedication. Especially when this help was paid for, we might see it as a transaction that does not require much second thought.

Sensing our interconnection as humans seems difficult. We are so different from each other, in our views, in our heritage, our culture. Our sense of identity is shaped as much by association with certain groups as it is by our disassociation from others. We might identify as American, German, Russian, French, British (add your nationality) and with that comes the whole story about what this means and how we are different from others. The same happens when we identify as Buddhist, Christian, Jewish, Muslim, Atheist or other. What we stand for is often directly related to what we do not stand for. Add to that our identification with our gender, skin color, education, or wealth and things become even more complex. Having a sense of self is a healthy psychological development. Knowing what we stand for is imperative if we are to lead authentically and effectively. The problem arises when we are so caught up in our illusion of a separate self that we start believing in our own superiority, dehumanizing another group and failing to see their basic human needs for safety, to be seen, and to be satisfied. Becoming aware of our stories that keep us disconnected allows us to take a step back and remember our common humanity.

Sensing our interbeing is the practice of recognizing and opening to both the suffering and the beauty in this world. Because our lives are deeply interconnected, we can feel the pain of others and, no matter how fortunate we may be, it affects us. We can choose to turn a blind eye, to not engage with the news, to distract ourselves with work and entertainment. But the consequence is further disconnection from ourselves and the world around us. To feel our pain, let alone the pain of this world, is hard. I remember a conversation I had with a respected physics professor, contemplating what it takes to motivate people to make a positive difference in the world. I said something about the need to cultivate compassion and feeling the pain in this world. He looked at me seriously. I already wondered if I had gone too far and expected a lecture about how naïve this view was and that the world is much more complex than that. Instead, he, a very rational and masculine man, looked at me and said, "But Susanne, if I could feel the pain of the children in Africa—I would go crazy, I could not do anything!"

It is true, sometimes looking at the pain in this world—the dehumanization, the violence, the wars, the injustices, hunger, modern day slavery, mass extinction, pollution of our waters and soil, ice caps melting much faster than expected—can be overwhelming and paralyzing. Perhaps you, too, felt deeply touched by recent news and images of war, violence, and destruction. When we turn toward the suffering in this world, the sheer scale of the problems can leave us feeling sad, angry, and helpless. Many of our current social and environmental issues are so complex that there is no one, easy solution. Sometimes, different perspectives may seem contradictory, but both can be true. It is exactly in this space of discomfort, of not knowing, of letting our hearts be cracked open by our pain and the suffering in this world, that we can learn to go beyond our dualistic thinking of good and evil, of us and them, and create change from a place of interbeing.

Because there are so many problems in the world and so much suffering, we must remember to also look for the beauty in this world. Usually, where there is a catastrophe, there are also helpers. There is care, solidarity, compassion, and generosity. We can also remember to enter the present moment, breathe, and be here right now. For many of us, there is a lot of goodness in our lives in this present moment. We can open to this goodness and let it nourish us, not to forget the pain but to expand our capacity to hold it. I meet a lot of people, especially so-called activists, who are so filled with grief and a sense of urgency that they risk burning out. Some people tell me that they feel they have no right to be joyful when others in different parts of this world are suffering so much. In my experience, this view is not helpful. We must be joyful, when we can. We must be peaceful, when we can. Because everything is interconnected, essentially in a web of relationships with others, our actions and ways of being impact others directly and indirectly. Embodying hope when times are desperate, courage when times are scary, love when the world seems at war, these are superpowers. Again, this is not a bypassing of either your pain or that of the world but strengthening your capacity to be with it all.

By cultivating an awareness of your interconnectedness with all things and embracing your interbeing, you can develop the inner capacity to be with both the challenges and the beauty of the world. Of course, our journey doesn't end here. In the upcoming chapters, I'll guide you to work with your thoughts and take concrete actions. Nevertheless, the initial steps involve grounding yourself in the present moment, contemplating your interdependence, and feeling it within your body. These foundational actions set the stage for creating change from a place of interbeing rather than separation. As we remember our interconnectedness with nature and humanity, we come to realize that the solutions we seek demand a profound reevaluation of our impact on this intricate web of relationships.

Individual and Collective Trauma

As you open up to the suffering around us, as well as to your own, you are likely to encounter trauma. The renowned psychologist, biophysicist, and trauma expert Dr. Peter Levine writes: "Trauma is about loss of connection—to ourselves, our families, and the world around us. This loss is hard to recognize because it happens slowly, over time."[45] Dr. Gabor Maté, psychologist, trauma expert, and holocaust survivor stresses the inner process. "Trauma is not what happens to you but what happens inside you."[46] It is the inner injury that happens from a hurtful event, for example the experience of an accident, the sudden loss of a loved one, abuse by a family member, an attack by a stranger, public humiliation, abandonment and neglect when we are in need.

Trauma can be experienced individually and collectively and both feed each other. Collective trauma refers to a traumatic psychological effect shared by a group, community, or society resulting from acute events or ongoing conditions, such as natural disasters, war, or systemic oppression. This type of trauma shapes our collective memory, influences cultural and societal norms, and can persist as a disruptive force within these larger structures for long periods of time where we perceive harm that is being done to certain types of people as normal.

Trauma is so prevalent that many times we don't recognize it because what we experience is considered normal or we have learned to "just get on with it." All of us have had a traumatic experience at some point in our lives. When an experience is traumatic and too much for us to process at the time, the triggered emotions are pushed into our subconscious so that we can continue to function. It is an intelligent survival response of our body. Because our experience is buried in the subconscious, it is possible that we are not aware of a trauma until years later when we experience either strong emotions or dullness and depression.

In the United States, it has been estimated that more than six hundred thousand children experience abuse each year. The most common form of abuse is neglect, followed physical abuse (16%) and sexual abuse (10%).[47] Nearly one in ten American children have seen a family member abuse another family member. One national survey finds more than two out of five women, as well as two out of five men, in the United States experience physical violence by an intimate partner in their lifetime. Even in peaceful times, in the absence of war, bombs, and gunshots, we make each other feel unsafe and unseen.

Whether an experience is traumatizing depends on our ability to process and integrate it. It could be a single shocking event or chronic exposure to traumatic events over time. In these situations, we often do not have the time or the capacity to process the strong and, consequently, overwhelming emotions. Common symptoms of trauma are being easily startled, being on constant alert, disassociating from our body, experiencing emotional numbness, and emotional and physical reactivity to reminders, holding negative beliefs about oneself or others, suffering loss of memory, and difficulty concentrating. The problem is that unhealed trauma keeps us stuck in the past, keeps us from feeling fully alive in our body, limits our ability to choose a response, and limits our ability to experience the world open-mindedly. As leaders of change, we aim to respond rather than react, see clearly instead of being confused, remain focused instead of getting distracted, act instead of feeling overwhelmed, spread love rather than fear, and sense our connection both within ourselves and with the world around us. In order to be able to do that, we need to do our inner work.

You may have noticed that sometimes family patterns seem to repeat themselves across generations. Indeed, research shows that children growing up in households with an alcoholic parent are four times more likely to abuse alcohol as adults. Similarly, it is not unusual that violent adults who are physically, psychologically, and sexually abusive grew up themselves being victims of such violence. There is increasing evidence that trauma experienced by our ancestors can be passed on to subsequent generations through epigenetic inheritance. Studies involving Prisoners of War and Holocaust survivors found that the subsequent generation showed increased symptoms of anxiety, depression, and symptoms of post-traumatic stress disorder (PTSD). An experiment with mice demonstrated that male mice who received small shocks in conjunction with the smell of cherry blossom, passed on a heightened sensitivity to that particular smell to their children and grandchildren[48] and other studies found epigenetic changes in worms even fourteen generations later.[49]

This is quite remarkable and yet another expression of our interbeing. Long after their death, the suffering of our grandparents, who often endured war, poverty, loss, violence, dominance, suppression, and persecution, can still affect us through ancestral trauma. Even without direct experience of the original trauma, as a child and grandchild of a trauma survivor you can carry emotional residues in your body that influence your behavior patterns, as well as your psychological and physical condition.

Not only are we affected by our own experiences and those of our ancestors, but as members of a certain community we are also affected by collective trauma. It is easy to see how these forms of trauma are intricately linked. Individual trauma can be a direct result of systemic issues related to collective traumas, like growing up in a war-torn society, growing up with racism, living with no rights as a woman, being publicly shamed for your sexual orientation, growing up in deep poverty, or being banished from your homeland. In turn, individual trauma might contribute to collective trauma, as personal narratives merge to form a shared understanding of events, conditions and social norms. Ancestral trauma bridges these domains, reminding us of our interbeing across time and space.

Considering the intricate links between our individual, ancestral, and collective traumas, it becomes evident that our inner work—such as becoming more mindful, tending to our internal wounds, reevaluating our belief systems, and reestablishing a connection with our hearts—serves not only our own wellbeing but also that of future generations. At the same time, our outer work, the way we run our businesses and organizations, how we relate to our family and community, can have a direct impact on the prevalence of individual trauma in this world. Both our inner and outer work are crucial in creating positive change.

Your Body Remembers

Just as your body is your gateway to the present moment, it is also where your individual, collective, and ancestral trauma is stored. Perhaps you are aware of a situation in your life that left a lasting inner injury, but you are doing your best to move on, to not feel the feelings, and to concentrate on the future. Or you are unaware of any such situation and still surprised how some situations seem to trigger a disproportionate amount of anger or fear when looked at rationally. Whether we are aware of our feelings or whether they are buried in our subconscious, they are held in our body (until we are able to release them).

I used to get easily startled; my mind is hypervigilant and involuntarily running one worst-case scenario after another. As a child I did not always feel emotionally and physically safe in my home. As an adult, I used to feel like my life could fall apart any minute, but I'd be ready for it; my body pumped up with adrenaline, my heart racing, my head spinning, and my Sympathetic Nervous System fully activated for large parts of my day. At night, I frequently woke up screaming, unable to remember my dream. Fear was running the show, day and night, and my body would feel tense and tired. It was exhausting.

When we have a traumatic experience, our nervous system typically engages in a fight, flight, or freeze response. Research shows that individuals with a history of chronic neglect or abuse often exhibit a dominance of the immobilization or shutdown response. In this freeze mode, life tends to feel like a strange movie, unreal and impersonal. Physical symptoms can range from a lowered heart rate, gastrointestinal issues, migraines, certain types of asthma, persistent pain, chronic fatigue, and a general withdrawal from life. In contrast, when we experience acute trauma, i.e., a singular event, our body tends to activate the fight or flight mode (our Sympathetic Nervous System), which manifests in an increased heart rate, shallow breathing, and a constant state of alertness.

It is important to remember that all three states are primal and healthy reactions as our body prepares to face a perceived threat. Historically, when confronted with a predator in a life-threatening situation in nature, our best response for survival would be to fight or flee from a predator. Sometimes freezing and playing dead would be the best lifesaving strategy. Which strategy to pursue is a primal automatic reaction in our Autonomous Nervous System and not an elaborate decision-making process, which would lead to our certain death. A healthy nervous system bounces back from its high-alert state and enters the parasympathetic rest and digest mode when back in a safe environment.

And yet, many of us live with a dysregulated nervous system. Remember that trauma is not the event that happens to you but what happens inside of you as a result of an experience, either leaving a lasting inner injury or not. When a situation is traumatizing, we stay in this state of heightened alert and chronic stress, or we become dull and disengaged. Even well after a traumatic event has passed, the slightest suggestion of threat can trigger a response, activating disrupted brain pathways and releasing a significant amount of stress hormones. This can lead to intense emotional distress, strong physical sensations, and sudden aggressive or overly fearful behaviors, which may feel like we are out of control. Unaddressed trauma can lead to lasting changes in various areas of your brain, such as the amygdala, which handles emotional responses, the hippocampus, crucial for memory and learning, and the prefrontal cortex, which plays a key role in decision-making and self-control. These changes can affect how you regulate your emotions, recall memories, and process information.

A chronic state of alertness creates a constant current of tension in our body and is generally quite uncomfortable. Consequently, as a society, we've become very good at escaping. Gabor Maté describes this aptly in his book *The Myth of Normal*:

> *"Work pressures, multitasking, social media, news updates, multiplicities of entertainment sources—these all induce us to become lost in thoughts, frantic activities, gadgets, meaningless conversations. We are caught up in pursuits of all kinds that draw us in not because they are necessary or inspiring or uplifting, or because they enrich or add meaning to our lives, but simply because they obliterate the present."*[50]

Our unacknowledged, unprocessed, and unintegrated history is a significant source of our personal and collective suffering. This pain often stems from the refusal to recognize, acknowledge, and integrate our past experiences. While at the time of the crisis, our disassociation from the body is an intelligent mechanism to help us cope with an unbearable situation, it is precisely the reconnection with our body that helps us to physically, emotionally, and mentally reintegrate the past. Trauma researcher Bessel van der Kolk concludes: "In order to change, people need to become aware of their sensations and the way that their bodies interact with the world around them. Physical self-awareness is the first step in releasing the tyranny of the past."[51]

Mindfulness has helped me to create the inner spaciousness and loving awareness that allowed me to be present with the uncomfortable sensations in my body. Somatic work, particularly breathwork, has helped me to transform and process subconsciously stored emotions. I still find it to be an effective practice to help release physical and emotional tension and process whatever needs to be processed to reconnect a sense of ease, love, and interbeing. Fear is still a visitor but it is no longer a permanent resident in my body.

However, there are circumstances when mindfulness and meditation may not be the right medicine, nor is it necessarily sufficient. When you are currently experiencing a traumatic situation, being with all the emotions and sensations can be too much. Similarly, ripping off the bandage of old traumatic wounds, when you don't have the capacity yet to be with the intense emotions, can also be counterproductive. In these cases, or whenever you feel stuck, please seek advice from teachers and professionals.

Healing and Regeneration

Our current way of living and working reinforces our sense of disconnection from ourselves, each other, and nature. Healing is about reestablishing that connection. By healing the past, we free ourselves from old patterns of thinking, feeling, and acting, which allows us to create a different kind of future. With mindfulness you can start to see more clearly and create the inner spaciousness that is needed to process previously stuck emotions in the body. Healing individual and ancestral trauma can break cycles of abuse and neglect, leading to more wholesome relationships personally, professionally, and as a community. This way, we find a path to reconnect with who we are and what matters. In turn, we can mend our relationships and we can create different organizational operating models that are in service to human and planetary wellbeing. Ultimately, I believe we can thereby prepare the ground from which a new way of living and being can emerge for humanity, one that is founded in wisdom and compassion.

Like so many things, our healing is non-linear and unpredictable. It might happen many times that you are done with a limiting belief, that you "healed your relationship with…" or that you finally decided to no longer blame your parents or partner or society for your experience. And then, all of a sudden, you are triggered again! Or you think you are never going to change, you are increasingly aware, you meditate, you pause and breathe, and still you seem to be unable to shake off that one particular stubborn habit. Then, one morning, you wake up and you no longer feel drawn to that habit. My experience has been that healing happens in layers. Like an onion, we peel off layer by layer, and each time we become a bit more free and loving.

Our inner work can only be done by ourselves but never alone; we need other people if we are to heal. Sometimes, others serve as a mirror to show us where we have more work to do. When someone or a certain type of person continually triggers us, it is an interesting opportunity to investigate the beliefs behind our reaction and the emotions that we don't want to feel. Other times, other people share their wisdom or talents to help us heal. Sometimes, it is a friend that creates the safe space we need in order to be able to see clearly and feel the emotions that need to be felt.

Peter Levine's definition of trauma underlines the importance of others in witnessing our pain: "trauma is not what happens to us, but what we hold inside in the absence of an empathetic witness." Already simply being with someone and listening to their story with compassion and without judgment can create an environment for healing. Collectively, we need to acknowledge the pain we have caused each other, particularly if it was systematically and politically inflicted by one group on another, for example. This is also why it is important to be able to have a conversation about historical systematic abuse and sometimes even killing of a certain type of people such as indigenous people, non-whites, women, homosexuals, religious groups, etc. We have seen the importance of being seen and heard in institutions such as the Truth and Reconciliation Committee in South Africa after the end of Apartheid. Sensing our interbeing across space and time we can see the violence and destruction that has been taking place and we can commit to a different path.

In addition to needing other people to help us heal, we also need nature. Many of us intuitively love spending time in nature. Whether we head to the park or countryside, go hiking in the mountains or for walks on the beach, nature helps us reconnect within ourselves. Nature has an incredible capacity to facilitate both mental and physical healing. When we immerse ourselves in natural surroundings, the soothing sights, sounds, and smells of the outdoors can alleviate stress, reduce anxiety, and improve our overall mental wellbeing. The simple act of taking a walk through a forest or sitting by a river can calm our minds, lower our blood pressure, and boost our mood. Animals and pets have a well-documented therapeutic effect and help us boost our mood, feel less lonely, and give us a sense of purpose.

Now nature needs us too. Our current resource consumption and production of waste leaves nature with little opportunity to regenerate itself. Consider the widespread deforestation and loss of biodiversity due to expanding agriculture. In many regions, forests have been cleared to make way for crops or livestock, pushing countless species to the brink of extinction and disrupting vital ecosystems. The time has come for a profound shift in mindset; it's no longer merely about implementing a sustainability strategy and being a little less bad. Instead, we must become, as the former Chairman of Unilever Paul Polman says, "net positive" by giving more than we take.[52] Regeneration intends to give nature the space and environment it needs to heal so that it can continue to nourish us.

Regeneration and healing are mutually reinforcing. As we start to heal the parts in us that feel disconnected, we become more alive and receptive to nature's beauty and its intelligence. Sensing our interbeing with all things can remind us that we are not alone, that there is an intelligence to life, and that the inner work we do has a direct outer impact. As we sense our interconnection and love for this life, including all living species, a natural desire arises to protect it and to become of service. Thus, by helping to restore nature, we are also restoring ourselves and can create a new story about what it means to be human.

Week 2–Going Deeper: Introduction to Regenerative Business

Regenerative business represents a paradigm shift in how companies approach their operations, growth, and impact on the world. Unlike traditional business models focused solely on profit maximization, regenerative business aims to restore, renew, and revitalize the surrounding ecosystems, communities, and economies. It is a holistic approach that emphasizes the interdependence of all life forms and systems. Regeneration moves beyond sustainability, which often seeks to do less harm, to actively improving and healing these systems.

Leading thinkers in this field include the entrepreneur and environmentalist Paul Hawken on Regeneration and Climate Change;[53] Daniel Christian Wahl on Regenerative Design;[54] Giles Hutchins and Laura Storm on Regenerative Leadership;[55] international advisor and lecturer Hunter Lovins, as well as former Managing Director at JP Morgan John Fullerton, on Regenerative Capitalism.[56, 57] To understand the potential impact of regenerative agriculture in restoring ecosystems and reversing climate change, I recommend watching the award-winning Netflix documentary *Kiss the Ground*.[58]

Principles of Regenerative Organizations

Regenerative organizations are designed around principles that encourage systemic health, resilience, and equitable value creation. These principles include:

1. **Holism**: Viewing the business as part of a larger living system, recognizing the interconnectedness of economic, social, and environmental factors.
2. **Evolutionary Purpose**: Aligning business goals with broader societal and ecological wellbeing, beyond just profit.

3. **Empowered Participation**: Encouraging active involvement and engagement from all stakeholders, fostering a culture of collaboration and innovation.
4. **Regenerative Value Creation**: Designing products and processes that meet human needs within planetary boundaries, design for biological cycle and ecosystem regeneration, including materials and circularity.
5. **Systems Thinking**: Understanding our economy and organizations as complex systems, addressing root causes rather than just treating symptoms, considering long-term impacts.

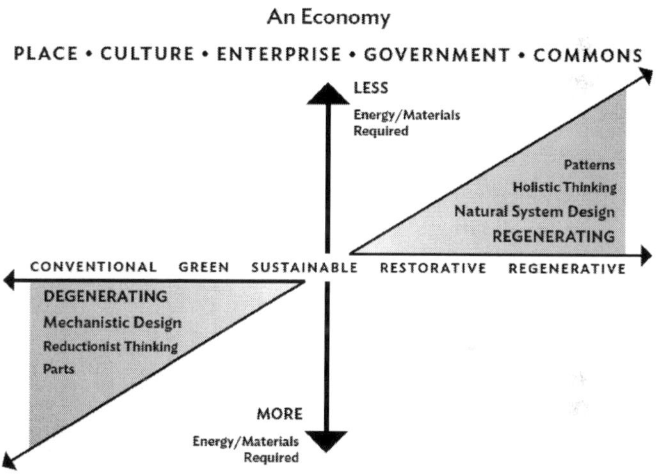

Moving from a conventional to a regenerative economy.
Credit: John Fullerton, Capital Institute, and Bill Reed, Regenesis Group

A Case Study: Patagonia

In 2022, Yvon Chouinard, Founder of Patagonia, the outdoor clothing and gear company with an estimated revenue of $US1.5billion,[59] set a precedent. After controlling the company's stock since its foundation fifty years prior, he transferred his family's ownership to a trust and non-profit and declared, "Earth is now our only shareholder."[60]

Since its foundation, Patagonia has been a pioneer in sustainability, integrating regeneration into its business model in several ways:

- **Environmental Impact**: Patagonia uses recycled and organic materials in its products, reducing its ecological footprint. The company's "Worn Wear" program encourages customers to repair, reuse, and recycle their gear.
- **Corporate Activism**: Patagonia campaigns for environmental causes, such as protecting public lands and addressing climate change. It donates 1% of its sales to environmental non-profits through the "1% for the Planet" initiative.
- **Supply Chain**: The company ensures fair labor practices and invests in sustainable agriculture, such as supporting regenerative organic farming methods that enhance soil health and biodiversity.

"The idea of ultimately running a regenerative business, that is the biggest idea that we're capable of, and we're a long, long way from realizing that," says CEO Ryan Gellert.[61] The journey is not without its challenges and contradictions, but Patagonia shows that even large businesses, in one of the most polluting industries, can pave the way and inspire business leaders who want to serve the wellbeing of this planet.

In summary, regenerative business offers a transformative approach where companies contribute to the wellbeing of nature and society. By adopting regenerative principles, businesses not only reduce their negative impacts but also actively contribute to the healing and flourishing of the ecosystems and communities they interact with. This shift toward regeneration holds the promise of a more resilient and equitable future, where business success is intertwined with the health of our planet and its inhabitants.

Underlining the inner process of creating outer impact, and my intention with this book, Daniel Christian Wahl writes that "creating regenerative systems is not simply a technical, economic, ecological or social shift: it has to go hand-in-hand with an underlying shift in the way we think about ourselves, our relationships with each other and life as a whole."[62]

Week 2–Questions and Exercises

Questions

- What do you notice about how you feel when you spend time in nature?
- Would you like to spend more time with nature and if yes, how could you do that?
- What are the conditions and moments in which you can best sense your interconnection with the world around you?
- How does collective trauma manifest in your line of work? Are you acknowledging this in the way you make decisions?
- What stories and beliefs have you inherited from your ancestors? How do they make you feel in your body?
- Is the social and environmental impact of your work net positive or negative?

Exercises

- This week, spend an hour or two alone in nature, observing and sensing your body. Switch your phone off, no music. Bring your awareness to your breath, feel your body, and expand your awareness to notice your surroundings. There is no need to analyze your experience; simply allow yourself to be in a relationship with nature and feel your body.
- Pause several times during your day, bringing your full awareness to your body and what is happening around you. Pick a moment when you are surrounded by people (it could be a small group or crowd). Observe the interaction. Can you sense their desire to be seen, to feel safe, and to be happy?
- Take time to reflect on the concept of interbeing (if you prefer another word like interdependence or interconnection, feel free to use it). How have different relationships shaped who you are today? How do you see humanity's role in the web of life and as part of nature? What does that mean for your role as a leader? Journal, if you find that helpful.

Week 2–Daily Meditation

Meditation on Interbeing

This week's meditation is designed to cultivate sensing our interbeing with others and nature. You can alternate this meditation with the *Meditation on the Body* from Week One.

Details about accessing this meditation can be found on my website.

https://www.susannevonderbecke.com/consciousimpact/meditation2

A transcript of this meditation can be found in the appendix.

Week 2–Optional Breathwork

Basic Diaphragm Breathing

This simple practice helps us to become more aware of our breath and to breathe deeper. Most of us breathe too fast and too shallow (mostly into the chest). This technique calms the breath and the mind. You can practice this by lying down, sitting, or standing.

1. Place one hand on your belly just beneath the rib cage. (If you like, place the other hand on your chest).
2. Slowly inhale through your nose, let your breath travel down your abdomen and feel your ribs expanding. Let your inhalation be gentle, don't force the expansion. You are taking slightly fuller and fewer breaths than you do normally. The stomach should push upward against your hand while the chest remains still.
3. Slowly exhale through your mouth with pursed lips. Make the exhalation slightly longer than the inhalation.

Practice for 3–5 minutes before your meditation or any time during the day.

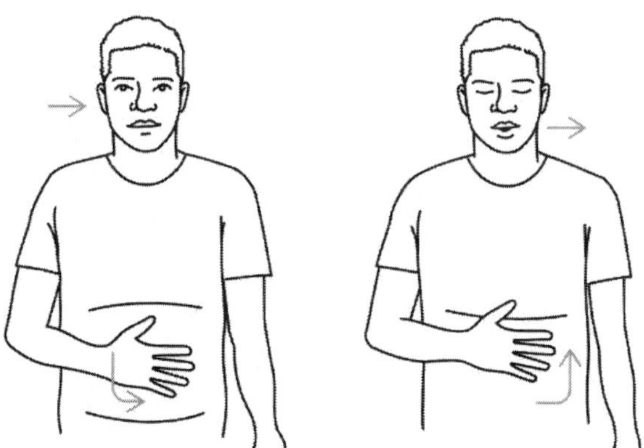

RECONNECTING ON THE LEVEL OF THE MIND

Having become more present and aware of your body, in the next two chapters you will learn to observe and investigate your thoughts and emotions. This meta-awareness is a crucial skill for moving from automatic reaction to conscious and deliberate response, especially in challenging situations. Becoming aware of our thoughts, feelings, and patterns is a first step toward a new freedom that enables us to act in alignment with who we want to be. Over time, we become more aware of how we've been shaped by our culture, our upbringing, our social status and the, often unconscious, beliefs they entail. By cultivating an open mind, we start seeing that the difficulties we encounter are also our pathway to inner and outer transformation. What is in the way, *is* the way. As we learn to accept both ourselves and the world as it is we create the inner spaciousness that is necessary for new ways of being to emerge. In this context, getting comfortable with discomfort is a key skill to be able to embrace uncertainty and reconnect to a sense of trust that helps to lead ourselves and others into the unknown.

LEADERSHIP SKILLS
FOR CONSCIOUS IMPACT
Chapter 3
Cultivating Presence & Awareness
Chapter 4
Sensing our Interbeing
Chapter 5
Cultivating an Open Mind
Chapter 6
Being Comfortable with Discomfort
Chapter 7
Cultivating an Open Heart
Chapter 8
Leading with Purpose

CHAPTER 5

WEEK 3 | CULTIVATING AN OPEN MIND

"We are what we think. All that we are arises with our thoughts. With our thoughts, we make the world."
Buddha

The deliberate cultivation of an open mind allows us to move beyond our habitual dualistic and linear way of thinking and create the inner spaciousness from which new solutions can emerge. This practice is not just about embracing diversity or tolerating differences; it's about fostering a new way of being that aligns with the principles of interconnectedness and mutual respect. An open mind is the gateway to understanding, enabling us to see beyond the confines of our individual experiences and appreciate the vast tapestry of life. It encourages us to live in harmony with the natural world, recognizing our role not as dominators but as stewards of the Earth. By cultivating open-mindedness, we pave the way for a more sustainable, compassionate and inclusive society, and regain our sense of wonder and appreciation for the beauty of life.

Have you ever met someone who describes themselves as closed-minded? I have not. I think most of us like to think of ourselves as open-minded, myself included. I think that I am a positive and open-minded person but when I question my beliefs honestly, I find plenty of moments where I am judgmental, invested in being right and not open to perspectives contradicting my own. Especially in roles where we feel the obligation to take the lead or when we feel we have to fight for justice, climate change, inequality, the erosion of values or whatever it is that sparks your fire, it is a balancing act to take a stand and be willing to be wrong and open to learning.

Despite the widespread belief in our own open-mindedness, the reality is that most of us exist in self-constructed bubbles. Our views are shaped not only by our upbringing, culture, and personal experiences but also significantly by technology, social media, and their algorithms. These digital platforms, while designed to connect us, often do the opposite by curating content that aligns with our existing views and preferences, further entrenching us in our ideological echo chambers. The bubbles thus become not just self-constructed but algorithmically reinforced, limiting our exposure to new ideas, perspectives, and ways of life even more. Being genuinely open-minded in this context requires a conscientious effort; it demands that we actively seek out and engage with thoughts and beliefs that challenge our own, both online and offline. It's a continuous process of unlearning and relearning, of being curious and embracing the Unknown.

The current state of the world requires us to find new solutions, new ways of living our lives, running our organizations and countries. As both enablers and inhibitors of change, it is crucial for each of us to understand our own mind. It is helpful to remind ourselves that our current laws, social norms and rules started with a system of beliefs about what is right and wrong. As we evolve in our understanding of interbeing, different norms and rules will emerge.

The concept of social rules as constructs of the mind is evident when we examine the historical context of many now-outdated laws and norms. For example, the prohibition against women voting was once a widely accepted societal norm, rooted in deeply ingrained beliefs about gender roles and capabilities. Similarly, laws criminalizing interracial marriages reflect past societal prejudices that, with time and open-mindedness, have been recognized as unjust. These examples highlight how social constructs can evolve, underscoring the importance of questioning and challenging the status quo. By acknowledging that many of our current norms and rules are also constructs that can be reevaluated, we open ourselves to the possibility of creating a more equitable and just society.

Finally, cultivating an open mind enables us to replace judgment with curiosity. It means approaching the Unknown not with fear or suspicion but with a desire to understand and learn. An open mind invites us to question our belief systems and the societal norms we take for granted. It encourages us to see mistakes not as failures but as opportunities for growth and learning. By fostering an open-minded approach to life, we build bridges between disparate ideas and communities, facilitating dialogue and understanding. An open mind is not just a personal asset; it is a tool for societal transformation, enabling us to envision and work toward a future that is more inclusive, compassionate, and connected.

Meeting Your Monkey Mind

When we begin the journey of mindfulness and turn our attention inward, it doesn't take long to observe that our mind rarely stays still. It jumps from thought to thought, much like a monkey swinging from tree to tree without pause. This is why in mindfulness we sometimes refer to our "monkey mind," the restless, incessant movement of our thoughts, emotions, and desires[63], jumping from one branch to another without a moment's rest.

This realization often leads to a common frustration among those new to meditation. Many times, I've heard people say: "Meditation? I tried that but it doesn't work for me." And when I ask, "What happened?" they usually respond "I keep having thoughts, I just can't stop thinking." This is probably the most common misconception about meditation, the idea that we can just shut off our thoughts. It ignores the very nature of our mind.

Having thoughts during meditation is not only normal, it also helps us to better understand ourselves, our own patterns and entanglements as well as the subtler truths in life such as impermanence, the existence of suffering, our desire to be happy, and interbeing. When observed with curiosity and kindness, our monkey mind can lead us to find wisdom and compassion. Rather than attempting to stop our thoughts, which is a futile endeavor, the aim is to cultivate a state of active, open attention to the present moment and observe our thoughts as they arise and pass, without getting caught up in their content. This way, we learn to collect the mind and as a result we will be able to see more clearly. This practice enables us to become aware of our thought patterns, including the biases and repetitive stories that dominate our mental landscape.

Studies suggest that the average person has about sixty thousand thoughts per day. A staggering fact is that a significant portion—some estimates suggest 90%—of these thoughts are repetitive. Moreover, many of these recurring thoughts are not necessarily based on facts or reality, indicating that much of our mental energy is consumed not only by 'old news' but also 'fake news' such as unfounded worries about the future. Studies have also shown that a wandering mind is an unhappy mind, that there is a direct correlation between rumination about the past or future and unhappiness.

Understanding Your Patterns

Fortunately, we have the amazing capacity to become aware of our thinking. We can remember to come back to the present moment, as you have been doing the last two weeks. We can get to know our typical patterns of thoughts and emotions and, by recognizing them, experience a whole new level of freedom.

During my teacher training, we were asked to observe our thoughts and write down the most frequent ones, our "Top 10 Tunes" playing like a musical hit parade in our heads. Firstly, I noticed that I am thinking all the time. I mean, *all the time*. I imagined that if I were to speak out loud every thought I was thinking, unfiltered, I would sound completely mad, or self-absorbed, or both. Remembering to hold my experience with curiosity and kindness, I started laughing. My mind, which I credit with certain capability of analytical thinking and having earned me a PhD no less, seemed to be completely untamed!

Identifying my top tunes, I learned that I tend to spend my time in the future, with planning, rehearsing, scenario thinking, etc. Now, you might think that does not sound too bad, perhaps better to think about the future in the name of planning than about the past with a sense of melancholy or regret. Of course, when leading our lives and being responsible in our organizations we need to plan for the future and run best- and worst-case scenarios. But my thoughts weren't limited to planning. In my mind, I would frequently run the absolute worst-case scenarios, preparing myself for the worst outcome. When a project was very important to me, I would see it fail before my eyes. I've lived through scenarios where the people I love most died in a car crash, where I sold our house to make ends meet, and where I would make a mistake and everything would fall apart. This type of thinking is called catastrophizing.

None of these terrible things ever happened. And you might be wondering, *Why on earth would she even want to imagine such scenarios?* Firstly, the thoughts come without an invitation. Second, I did not stop them because catastrophizing gave me a sense of control as I could feel prepared for the worst. Imagining my worst fears would in a bizarre way give me a sense of security. However, it would also make me feel terrible and hijack my nervous system to be in continuous fight or flight mode. Because these scenarios were always fear-based, this way of thinking took away my ability to stay open to what was really happening and be creative in finding solutions.

Becoming aware of my thoughts and emotions and noticing my automatic reactions to them helped me to understand this pattern and not let it influence my actions. As I have learned to get more comfortable with the fear of failure and loss, these catastrophic scenarios appear much less often. And when they do, I can see them coming and get to choose if I really want to engage with them or redirect my mind to a more helpful way of thinking.

We each have our unique stories and conditioned patterns to discover, yet there are certain biases and tendencies that we all share. Additionally, our personality influences our behavior and thought patterns. Buddhist psychology identifies three main personality types, the Greedy, Aversive, and Deluded. My catastrophic thinking described above is typical for the aversive type. While their description is, of course, a stylized generalization, I have found these types useful in being aware of my own tendencies as well as improving my compassion and empathy toward those wired differently.

As you read through the three types, keep in mind that we all have elements of each in us. For example, although I identify most with the Aversive type, I certainly have also experienced greed and delusion or confusion. The point is not to illustrate what is wrong with us but to highlight our default patterns so that we can turn them into the strength with which we can serve the world. Each of these personality types bears a gift of transformation.

Those with a Greedy disposition are often caught in the whirlpool of desire, their eyes alight with the shimmer of what's just beyond reach. This thirst isn't just for the material—though that's part of it—but for experiences, sensations, and connections that promise a taste of fulfillment. The greedy types have a natural ability to see beauty in life. When evaluating projects, they easily focus on opportunities while tending to overlook the risks. Since they like everything to be pleasant, they have a gift for creating harmonious places and communities. However, they can also have the tendency to gloss over difficult situations. In their constant quest for more, the greedy types can miss the richness of the present as they lose themselves in dreams gilded with 'if only'. However, when transformed, this type gives rise to beauty and abundance.

Then there are the Aversive types, also referred to as the Angry type, who walk the world with shields raised and swords drawn, ready to parry blows that haven't yet been dealt. To them, life's unpredictable ebbs and flows can seem like a series of potential threats that must be neutralized or avoided. Their minds are often critical and judgmental, quick to identify problems and assess risks. In meetings, this type thrives on directness and is not afraid of conflict. They hold the group to high standards of integrity and quality, speaking their truth and skillfully addressing challenges. As they tend to focus on everything that is, or could go, wrong with a situation, they can inadvertently turn away from the very experiences that hold the potential for growth and fail to grasp opportunities when they arise. The gift of transformation for the aversive personality is discerning wisdom, non-contentiousness, and loving-kindness.

Amid these, the Deluded or confused souls find themselves often lost in a fog of confusion and uncertainty. Reality, with all its complexity and nuance, seems a puzzle whose pieces they find difficult to fit together. This can make them feel unsure about what to do and how to relate to the world. When discussing a project in a meeting, it can take them longer to process the opportunities and risks involved and to figure out how they feel about something. Generally, they tend to orient themselves according to the opinions of others. They possess a natural beginner's mind, a certain innocence and openness that allows them to approach life with curiosity and receptivity. When things go wrong, they have the tendency to 'check out' and to not engage. The deluded temperament tends to be mellow and easy going. Without training of the mind, this type can miss the clarity and attention to detail that makes them feel fully alive and awake. However, when transformed, it gives rise to spaciousness, equanimity, and deep understanding.

Each personality type, with its challenges and insights, invites us to look deeper, to cultivate the opposite virtues—generosity, loving-kindness, and wisdom—and to find in our struggles the seeds of our liberation and offer them as a gift to the world.[64]

There are common thought patterns that many of us share, independent of our personality type. Some of them are a result of how our human brains evolved in order to detect danger early and survive (our negativity bias and automatic judgment). Others seem to me a typical conditioning in our individualistic and productivity-oriented cultures. For our journey as changemakers, I found it particularly useful to be aware of the following thought patterns:

- **Negativity bias**: the tendency to pay more attention to negative information or experiences than positive ones. This can lead to a skewed perception of reality both in relation to ourselves and the problems of the world.
- **Judgment**: the tendency to quickly label an experience as good or bad. It is often the voice of our inner critic who happily judges both ourselves and the people around us. This can make it harder for us to appreciate both the diversity and complexity of life and to see things from multiple perspectives.

- **Selfing**: the tendency to think that our world revolves around us. We like hearing ourselves and find pleasure in being Liked (literally, when checking our phones) by others. We also tend to take things personally or believe that events are directly related to us, even when they are not. In conversation with other people, it narrows our focus and can lead us to care more about being right than getting it right.
- **"Have to"**: characterized by a belief that there are fixed rules one must follow, creating a sense of compulsion or obligation that can lead to stress and anxiety. We feel pressured by perceived duties and responsibilities that may not actually be as rigid or obligatory as we believe.
- **"Should"**: often an indicator of situations when we are in resistance to our present-moment experience; we think it should be different because we wish it to be different. When the realities of our behavior, that of others, or the state of the world does not align with our expectations, we often react with guilt, frustration, and dissatisfaction. This increases our sense of separation from the world and narrows our focus to see primarily what is wrong with it.

Remember that it is normal that we have certain biases and thought patterns. For example, our negativity bias is a result of how our human brains have evolved and what helped our ancestors to survive. It was much more important for their survival to notice the tiger in the bush that might pounce on them if overlooked than to notice the beauty of the sunset. Even today, these patterns serve a purpose. Having an inner map of how our world works and being able to automatically judge what is good and what is bad for us is essential in most everyday circumstances. For example, we don't have time to consider all the complexities involved each time we make ourselves a cup of coffee or tea. However, if we want to solve complex challenges, it is helpful to refrain from automatic judgment and study the situation open-mindedly. Similarly, thinking in *shoulds* can help us to adhere to a particular value system and inspire us into action if we believe the reality is out of alignment. However, *only* thinking in *shoulds* will leave us frustrated and unable to create change from a state of openness.

The invitation here is not to get rid of our thinking patterns but to become wise about how we use our mind. As our thoughts trigger emotions that lead to actions, the more that we are aware of what we think, our mental shortcuts, and our stories in our minds, the better leaders we can become. Understanding your patterns will help you to become more free of the habitual thinking that keeps you chained to a version of yourself that is not in alignment with who you want to be.

No Bad Feelings

What makes unraveling our patterns so challenging is that our thoughts and our emotions are intertwined. How you think influences your feelings and your feelings influence what you think. The term emotion comes from the Latin word *emovere* which means *to excite* or *to stir up* in response to stimuli. Emotions move us into action. Our interpretation, how we think about our emotions, translates into feelings, which in turn can lead to longer-lasting moods. Especially in challenging situations, we can easily get stuck in repetitive feedback loops and navigating our inner landscape can feel like being lost in a dense forest without a map. To make things worse, much of our thought process is unconscious, which makes an awareness of our patterns even more important. It's been estimated that 95% of the thoughts influencing our actions are subconscious, although I have not seen any scientific evidence of that. Whatever the exact number is, unless we are mindful, our thoughts and emotions can lead us to act in ways that are harmful to ourselves or others and not in alignment with who we want to be.

However, you can learn how to navigate your inner landscape and find your inner compass when you feel lost. Before I explain the process of working with your thoughts and emotions, I want to point out one more thing that mindfulness taught me, which revolutionized how I think about positivity, self-improvement, and the true meaning of inner growth.

We think of our thoughts and emotions as either bad or good. For example, pessimism, sadness, and disappointment are often regarded as negative feelings; and optimism, cheerfulness, and satisfaction as positive ones. As leaders, we often strive to do our best and think that with enough self-improvement (a.k.a. discipline) we will be able to always 'think positively' and create a life full of positive experiences. We strive to optimize our work, personal life, and ourselves. While this can reflect personal growth, constantly judging our experiences as good or bad can trap us in resisting the present moment as it is, precluding the openness needed to learn, embrace and appreciate life as it unfolds.

The more empowering alternative suggests noticing whether an experience is pleasant, unpleasant, or neutral. In mindfulness, these three feeling tones (Vedanās) arise as a result of our inner and outer experiences. These tones describe the initial, often subconscious, emotional response we have to any stimulus, setting the stage for more complex feelings and thoughts to unfold. For example, experiencing a sound during your meditation can be a neutral experience, if you don't mind it. It can also be pleasant, if you like the sound, or unpleasant, if you dislike it. Whether a sound is barely noticeable, beautiful, or jarring depends on who experiences it: it is entirely subjective and depends on the circumstances. This can be true also for our emotions. For example, sadness can be experienced as depressing and disabling and it can also be the somewhat pleasant trembling in our heart when we remember someone we love. Similarly, anger, greed, and confusion are not necessarily good or bad; what matters is how we react to them.

Thinking of our experiences in terms of pleasant, unpleasant, and neutral allows us to keep an open mind and avoid the moral judgment that can keep us stuck in dualistic thinking and harmful feedback loops. With mindfulness, you will start to notice how your body and mind naturally contract when you feel uncomfortable and expand when you feel comfortable. You will notice that you do not pay much attention to neutral experiences, that you want more of the pleasant and try to avoid the unpleasant. With practice, you can cultivate an inner spaciousness, both physically and mentally, that will help you to relax into the discomfort. It will help you to be with challenging thoughts and emotions without pushing them away and consequently to let them go more easily. Similarly, you'll also learn to appreciate pleasant sensations without becoming overly attached to them, understanding that these, too, are temporary. This way you can rise to difficult situations with a whole new sense of empowerment.

Working with Thoughts and Emotions

When working with your thoughts and emotions, my first invitation is to bring a sense of curiosity and playfulness to your experience. A lot of the work is about feeling what we do not want to feel and letting go of thoughts that no longer serve us. It is as much about learning as it is about unlearning. Think of it as an adventure and ongoing work that allows us to become more authentic and cultivate the open-mindedness that allows new ideas and new ways of being to emerge.

Because our thoughts and emotions are intertwined and often feed each other, the situation dictates whether you work with your thoughts, or with your emotions, or with both. Working with your mind requires you to not believe everything you think. Working with your emotions requires you to feel everything that is safe for you to feel at the time. The practice you have been doing for the last two weeks, reconnecting with your body and becoming aware of your present-moment experience, is the basis for what comes next.

You can work with your thoughts and emotions as part of your meditation practice. And you can continue to train to notice and do your inner work during everyday life situations at work and at home. You always start with the same four steps:

Step 1: Notice

Remember to stay present and notice what is happening inside of you, either in response to outer stimuli (sounds, a smell, something you see) or inner stimuli (physical pain, a recurrent thought).

Step 2: Observe

Take a step back and observe what is happening. Instead of being trapped inside your thinking and feeling, you can observe *I am having the thought that… I am experiencing the emotion of…* Note the difference between thinking *I am disappointed* and thinking *I am experiencing disappointment*. The latter creates more spaciousness, a broader perspective that reminds you that you are not your thoughts or emotions. You can bring in the feeling tones, noticing whether your experience is *pleasant, unpleasant, or neutral.* This can help you to meet your experience with a sense of compassion because it's a reminder of your natural instinct to want to feel good. Another proven strategy to help you stay in the position of being an observer is to *name your experience.* When you are caught up in thinking, you can name the kind of thinking: remembering, planning, rehearsing, scenario thinking, blaming. Similarly, you can name your emotions, such as restlessness, nervousness, worrying, numbness, impatience, excitement, joy, calmness, etc.

Step 3: Let be

Before you can let go of anything, you must let be. For your *thoughts*, this means that you don't enter your train of thought, you stay outside, as if you were sitting on a hill and watching a train passing by. It is quite possible that your mind will come up with an enticing commentary about the color or shape of the train, its speed, whether it is pretty or not, or whether it should or shouldn't be there. That, too, is just another train that can pass by. If, despite your best intentions, you find yourself on the train, smile and remember to take back your position on the beautiful hill, watching it pass by. When an *emotion* arises, allow yourself to feel it. Sometimes it can be located in a specific area in your body, then let your breath help you to create spaciousness right there. Relax as much as you can into the sensation. Every thought or emotion is a temporary experience. It arises and, naturally, also disappears again—unless we resist it. This is why you cannot *let go* of anything that you have not previously allowed *to be.* (Note that this part of the practice is sometimes described as 'allowing'. I find that for some people 'allowing' evokes a sense of having to give permission, which can trigger more thoughts and emotions. In contrast, 'letting be' emphasizes the non-doing aspect of this practice and can be more neutral. Feel free to choose whatever wording you find most helpful.)

Step 4: Nourish

When experiencing a difficult emotion, it can be helpful to resource yourself. For example, if you are feeling worry, you might invoke a sense of trust; if you are feeling shame, you can bring in kindness and self-compassion. Taking a few deep breaths, going for short walk in nature, or connecting with a friend can help you to reset your nervous system.

These steps can be your go-to practice in any situation. Even though I wrote this in a particular order, in reality it is a more continuous practice of moving in and moving out, of noticing, observing, and letting be (allowing), observing again, noticing, nourishing (resourcing). After a while, you will feel what is needed and will be able to consciously direct your attention and create openness and insight.

There will be situations when you will feel stuck, where nothing naturally appears and dissolves. You resist feeling whatever is lurking behind your thoughts and your thoughts race uncontrollably. Instead of watching anything passing by it feels as if you are stuck on a high-speed run-away train, and that it is impossible to jump off. This is an opportunity for you to start investigating. Now is the time to bravely sit with whatever holds you back, uncovering and turning around limiting beliefs, processing emotions that keep you stuck in the past and hinder you from creating the future you want.

When you notice or suspect outdated beliefs and unprocessed emotions hold you back from responding the way you wish, you can set aside time to sit with this, investigate, and untangle your thoughts and emotions. First, find a place where you can be undisturbed and feel comfortable. Start by reconnecting with your body, taking a few deep breaths, and bringing your attention to the present moment. When you feel centered, think of the issue or situation you want to investigate and use the following questions to guide your investigation. Try not to get lost in your analysis. Continue to notice, observe and, most of all, feel.

What emotions are present? This question invites introspection into our emotional landscape, encouraging us to identify emotions we are avoiding about a situation. Often, we resist certain emotions because they are uncomfortable or painful, leading us to suppress or ignore them. However, by consciously acknowledging these emotions, we can begin to process them instead of allowing them to silently influence our actions and mindset. Many times, our emotions are fueled by our thinking and the assumptions we make about a situation. As we feel the emotions and examine our beliefs about a particular situation, we may uncover deeper layers of emotions to be acknowledged and felt. For example, we might initially feel anger in response to a situation, but as we allow this anger to be felt, we may discover an underlying emotion of grief.

What am I believing? This question helps us to uncover the underlying beliefs that shape our perception of ourselves, others, and the world around us. These beliefs, often formed in childhood and by our culture, can significantly influence our thoughts and behaviors. For example, beliefs like *I have to be the best so that...* , or *I can only be happy when...* may have helped us to achieve great things but on closer inspection they may keep us from living with more joy and ease. By examining the beliefs that guide our reactions and decisions, we can identify those based on past experiences that may no longer serve us. This awareness creates an opportunity to challenge and change limiting beliefs, thereby transforming how we interact with the world and enhancing our overall wellbeing.

Is this thought true? Do you know for sure that a particular thought is true? Asking ourselves the validity of our thoughts or beliefs encourages critical examination of their accuracy. Many of our beliefs and the stories we tell ourselves are not based on current reality but are rather interpretations or assumptions that can be distorted by our fears and past experiences. By scrutinizing the truthfulness of these beliefs, we can distinguish between what is factually based and what is a product of our subjective interpretation. This discernment helps reduce the power of unfounded beliefs and assumptions, allowing us to respond to situations with more clarity and less bias.

Is this thought helpful? This question prompts us to consider the utility and impact of our beliefs and emotions on our wellbeing and life goals. Even if a belief is true, it may not necessarily be beneficial to hold onto if it limits our potential or contributes to our suffering. Or it may simply not be helpful right now and something that you want to come back to later. By evaluating the helpfulness of our thoughts, we can make a conscious choice to adopt perspectives and attitudes that support our growth, happiness, and resilience. This pragmatic approach encourages us to focus on constructive and empowering beliefs, fostering a more positive and adaptive mindset.

Sometimes just sitting with these questions is enough to create a sense of spaciousness and an open mind. Especially when you are able to allow yourself to feel what is asking to be felt, without losing yourself in a narrative of thought and judgment as to whether this is good, bad, okay, allowed, or not. Meeting these emotions with loving-kindness is often all that is needed.

Finally, when you've investigated your thoughts, and you have felt your emotions, but still the same kind of unhelpful and untrue thoughts keep playing in your head, influencing your feelings and your actions, then there are three steps you can take.

1. **Stop:** Sometimes, when we have the same tune playing over and over again and we know it is not helpful and perhaps not even true, we simply have to say *Stop! I see you, I heard you but now it's enough*. Or *I release this pattern now!* Find the words that are most helpful to you. When you know that this thought does not have your best interests in mind and that you are listening for the hundredth time to it telling you that you are not doing enough, that you are not disciplined enough, or not worthy enough, then it is time to stop. And it works. Once you are aware enough to notice what tune is playing and you can distance yourself from it by sensing yourself as the observer, you have the capacity to decide to stop and think of something else. You might have to do that multiple times, but the less you keep firing the same neurons in your head, the weaker their connection will get and your tune will start to come less frequently.

2. Replace: When our thoughts are unhelpful, or we uncover limiting beliefs that are outdated, we can replace them with something helpful instead. Sometimes, this can look like moving from a limiting mindset to a growth mindset, for example, replacing *I don't have enough time* with *I prioritize what is important to me*. Sometimes, this can be to cultivate thoughts that are in alignment with our values and what matters to us. For example, practicing gratitude, and deliberately noticing what is good in our life and in this world, can counterbalance our inherent negativity bias and significantly improve our wellbeing and effectiveness as a leader.

3. Let go: Finally, sometimes we need to make the deliberate decision to let go. This is a tricky one because you cannot *let go* before you *let be*. When you really want something that is very important to you, for example, a promotion to give you more status and influence, or to become a loving parent, or to receive funding for your project, it is impossible to get yourself to 'just' *let go* and not want it anymore without giving up. What you can do, however, is to create the inner space to let go of obsessing about it. The steps described above can help, as can being outside in nature, doing your favorite sports, or listening to music. In that sense, letting go also involves stopping, replacing, and nourishing. Letting go is not only about obsessing about a future outcome, it can also mean letting go of the wish for a better past. In that instance, we may feel called to actively work with forgiveness (which we will explore more deeply in the next chapter).

Doing this investigative inner work takes time and often multiple repetitions. It is a powerful practice to help us focus on what truly matters and uncover limiting beliefs about ourselves, others, and the world. Gradually, we become a little more open and free. While there are certain steps you can follow, these practices are more an art than a science. What I have described above is a toolbox and with practice you will become very good at knowing which tools work best for you in a given situation. Our continuous practice in any situation is to notice, observe and let be, feeling what is asking to be felt and becoming ever more alive.

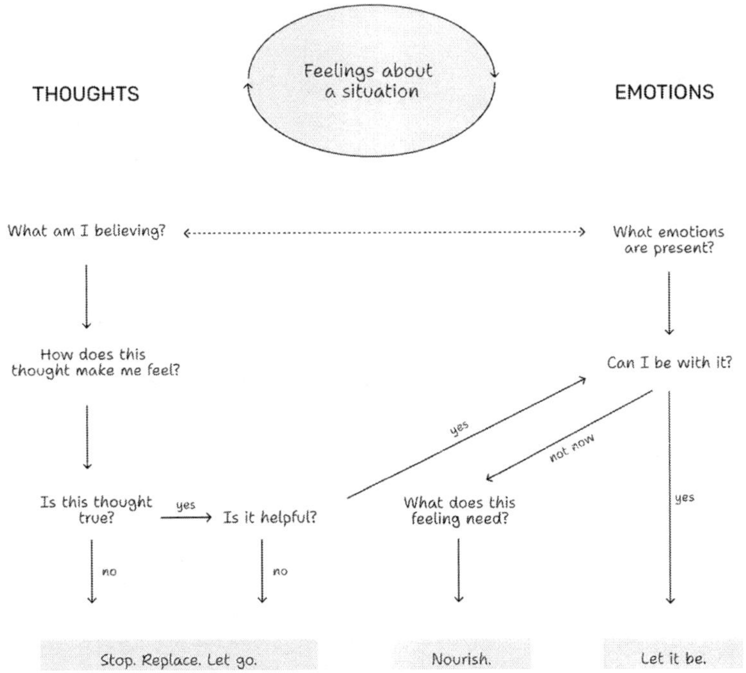

Working with thoughts and emotions when feeling stuck

No Mud, No Lotus

We are emotional beings and the more we become alive the more we care about this world. Although I find much beauty in this experience, it is not easy. Sometimes, our emotions can be so intense that we do not want to open up to them–it feels too much. Both the pain and the beauty can feel too much. Especially when trauma is involved, you want to create enough of a safe space for you to feel. The practice is a careful dance between allowing ourselves to feel and not overwhelming our nervous system, to build our resilience and steadiness amid the natural ups and downs of life.

It is important to understand that what is IN the way IS the way. We don't learn how to work with our thoughts and emotions to control our feelings. We work with them so that we learn to relax into the discomfort and transform fear into love. This way, we can effect outer change not only by what we do but how we do it. Our inner practice is to welcome all feelings, learn from them, heal from them and open ourselves up to the amazing experience of being a human being on this planet.

If you were given the possibility to spend the rest of your life connected to a virtual reality where you could experience all your dreams coming true and feel happy all the time, would you do it? You could experience anything you want, write your own script of life, make friends, be successful, change the world, there would be no failures, no humiliation, no doubt, no fear, etc., if you did not want it. Everything would feel real to you but physically you would stay in the same place connected to this virtual reality.

A similar question was asked by the American Harvard Philosopher Robert Nozick in the 1970s where people had the hypothetical choice to hook up to an experience machine where our life could be pre-programmed with only pleasurable experiences. The point of this question was to illustrate that we would not choose to be hooked up to this machine because humans after all do not value the pursuit of happiness over everything else. Interestingly, this thought experiment is now becoming a real possibility, where technology allows us to 'check out' and we don't have to deal with the emotional difficulties of our lives, unmet expectations and conflicts at work and at home.

We may have differing reasons why we would not sign up for this virtual reality that promises constant pleasure. Ultimately, I believe it comes back to our desire to feel part of the greater whole, that we find meaning in our connection with others and the natural world. There is beauty and wisdom to be found in difficult emotions. Just as the phrase "No mud, no lotus" describes, the lotus flower needs the mud in order to grow and bloom.[65] Our path to happiness and wisdom involves navigating difficulties and experiencing them is an important and valuable part of our journey. Hence, our practice is to welcome all emotions with a sense of curiosity and compassion.

This is easier said than done. As the Harvard Medical School Psychologist and author of *Emotional Agility* Susan David said, "you don't get a meaningful career or raise a family or leave the world a better place without stress and discomfort. Discomfort is the price of admission to a meaningful life."[66] Letting ourselves feel the discomfort, questioning our own modus operandi and assumptions about life takes courage and can leave us feeling vulnerable. However, as the professor and researcher Brené Brown finds, there is no courage without vulnerability. The good news is that, as you strengthen your ability to be with painful emotions, you also strengthen your capacity to be with positive emotions. It is impossible to suppress only the uncomfortable emotions and fully experience pleasurable emotions. Brown finds that "vulnerability is the birthplace of love, belonging, joy, courage, empathy, and creativity. It is the source of hope, empathy, accountability, and authenticity. If we want greater clarity in our purpose or deeper and more meaningful spiritual lives, vulnerability is the path."[67]

A Closer Look at Grief, Anger, Anxiety, and Shame

A few years ago, after I gave a talk during a mindful morning session at the conference of an environmental forum which I have been supporting, a participant came up to me. He was going to be on stage soon, leading a panel of experts on food systems and biodiversity, and said, "I am thinking about starting with a few minutes of silence. I feel so much grief, so much sadness [about the state we are in]." I told him that I did not think people were ready to do so and that this was not the right situation to try but I knew exactly what he meant. For leaders who want to create positive change and hence look at the problems of this world, wanting to find solutions, grief is a natural reaction. Other common emotions that I have experienced on my own journey and that have come up during my conversations with changemakers and business leaders are anger, anxiety, and shame. Let's take a closer look to understand what may be going on and how these difficult emotions can serve us.

- **Grief** touches the very core of our being. It is love with no place to go. This profound emotion is rooted in loss and carries within it an incredible capacity for transformation. Grief reminds you that everything is impermanent and that life is precious. When you face grief—whether from personal loss, witnessing the suffering of those around you, or confronting the vast challenges of our times—you're encountering a raw, unfiltered expression of love. It's a love that, in the face of absence, seeks new outlets, new ways to manifest and make a difference. This process, though painful, is a testament to the depth of your connections and the strength of your commitments. It propels you, as a leader, to honor what has been lost by dedicating yourself even more fervently to causes that foster life, healing, and peace.

The transformative power of grief lies in its ability to break down barriers—both within ourselves and among and between us. In acknowledging our collective losses and aspirations, grief can become a catalyst for solidarity, driving actions that are rooted in love, compassion, and a deep sense of interconnectedness.

- **Anger** is often misconstrued as purely destructive but carries within it a potent force for change. This intense emotion, when understood and channeled correctly, can serve as a powerful catalyst for action. When you feel anger bubbling up, it is a signal that something you deeply care about is under threat or has been violated. This emotional response is not just a personal grievance; it is a call to action, a demand for justice and rectification.

  Anger, when approached with awareness and intention, can sharpen your focus and lend urgency to your cause. It can motivate you to challenge the status quo, to stand up against injustices, and to fight tirelessly for the values you believe in. However, the true power of anger in leadership lies in its potential to inspire rather than alienate, to unite rather than divide. By modeling how to express anger in ways that are constructive and aimed at solutions, you pave the way for more effective and compassionate forms of advocacy.

- **Anxiety** is a feeling all too familiar in our fast-paced and uncertain world. While fear is a healthy response to potentially dangerous situations, anxiety is the state of constantly being afraid of what may happen in the future. Looking at the problems in the world, we are well aware of the scenarios that are likely to happen if humanity is not acting fast enough. Feeling anxious is a natural response but it narrows our focus and ability to seek novel solutions. At the same time, we feel under constant pressure to perform and as leaders of organizations are expected to anticipate and mitigate risks. While the occasional experience of anxiety is inevitable, being constantly anxious leaves us depleted and unable to experience the beauty of life. When uncontrolled, anxiety can leave us feeling powerless and depressed.

Anxiety asks us to find our way back from disconnection to connection. When we are anxious, we are not present and experience a sense of disconnection from ourselves and the world around us. We don't feel safe. We are lost in a hypothetical future that scares us. Sometimes, we don't feel particularly worried but we experience a constant state of alertness in our nervous system. Transforming anxiety is an invitation to reconnect with your body, people you love, nature, meaningful work, and a sense of agency.[68] It asks us to muster the courage to heal our inner wounds and reconnect to a sense of wholeness and belonging.

The gift of anxiety lies in the ability to anticipate and prepare for future challenges. By acknowledging and exploring your anxieties, you can turn them into a source of strength, using them to drive forward-thinking strategies and create more resilient and adaptable organizations. By sharing your own experiences with anxiety, you foster a culture of openness and support, encouraging others to voice their fears and work collaboratively toward overcoming them. This collective vulnerability builds trust, fosters empathy, and strengthens teams to better handle and recover from difficult situations.

- **Shame** makes us feel small and unworthy. It comes up when we fall short of our own expectations and deem ourselves unlovable. In a culture of not enoughness (not having enough, not being enough, not doing enough) this feeling is all too prevalent. Shame is one of the primary emotions and it is rarely helpful for creating positive change. It doesn't make us work harder or motivate us. Instead, our sense of self-esteem shrivels and without mindfulness it can easily trigger negative behavioral cycles.[69]

Another situation where shame comes up is in our identification as a victim or a perpetrator. Victims of abuse often wonder how they could let this happen to them and whether they were in any way complicit in making that violation happen. They are ashamed of telling anybody what happened. Similarly, we experience shame as a perpetrator, when we realize that we hurt another being but in a way that is not morally justifiable to us and is not in alignment with who we want to be. As a consequence, we feel ashamed and think we are a bad person.

Shame is also associated with societal values and our inherent need to belong. As we want to avoid feeling shame and want to be part of a group, shame keeps us in line and teaches us what is acceptable in a particular society and what is not. As leaders of change we don't always belong to the majority and tend to think differently from what is generally considered acceptable. In this instance, shame can be a catalyst to deepen our understanding of the values that truly matter to us. This way shame can become a profound source of personal growth and understanding. As a leader, confronting our shame—not as a mark of failure but as a step toward greater authenticity and compassion—can inspire those around us to do the same.

The gift of shame is its invitation to remember our inherent goodness and to feel worthy, regardless of our performance and of the expectations of others. It asks us to cultivate compassion for ourselves and others, to forgive mistakes and create the inner spaciousness that allows us to hold our human experience with loving presence.

Week 3–Going Deeper: Inquiry to Transform Limiting Beliefs

This 5-Step inquiry process will help you transform limiting beliefs that keep you stuck and hold you back from being the leader you want to be. A limiting belief is often fear-based and a statement about how the world is, how others are, and how we are. When a particular emotion comes up often or a situation seems to repeat itself again and again, it is quite possible that underneath you will find a limiting belief. There may also be limiting beliefs that you are well aware you have not yet been able to shake off. The 5-Step process below played a key role in overcoming my fear (panic is more accurate) of public speaking and unraveling unhelpful beliefs about myself, my marriage, and what success means to me. This process of inquiry is an adaptation of the work of my teacher Tara Brach[70], and of Byron Katie[71].

Find a quiet place to work where you feel safe and can be undisturbed. Make your favorite cup of tea or get some water, grab pen and paper[72], and follow the instructions below. Go through each of the questions and write down your answer. Take your time and make sure you are fully present. You will need about 20 to 30 minutes.

Write down your limiting belief

If you are not quite sure what it is but you keep getting stuck with the same emotions, you can ask yourself first: *What am I believing?*

Step 1
Do I know 100% that it is true? (If it is 100% true, it generally is an objective truth and not a belief.)

Step 2
What does it feel like to live with this belief? (Repeat the belief in your mind, remember situations from the past, notice any emotions arising and where you feel them in your body.)

Step 3
What does this feeling need? (There is usually unmet need underneath the belief. Tune into your body, keep an open mind and heart to whatever arises.)

Step 4
How did this belief serve me in the past? Is there any reason not to let go of it now? (Some beliefs served a purpose because they protected us. Whether this one did or not, write down if you are ready to let go.)

Step 5
How would it be to live without this belief? *Who would I be?* (Imagine what you would do and how you would feel.)

Write down your new belief

Rewrite what you chose to believe instead. It should feel empowering and aligned with what truly matters to you.

Note

You may want to revisit this work in the future. I like to keep a journal with these questions and my answers. My experience is that our old beliefs usually don't disappear in one go but that it gets easier to remember that they are not true when they arise. Each time, the old belief has a little less power until the new belief becomes our second nature. It can be interesting to go back and read your answers to a belief that has come up again after some time. Or you might discover beliefs that you had worked on and that you forgot you even had.

Week 3–Questions and Exercises

Questions

- Why does cultivating an open mind matter to you? What helps you to notice when you are closed-minded?
- What behavioral pattern described by the three personality types (greedy, aversive, deluded) resonates most with you?
- How does this pattern impact how you approach creating positive change in the world and at home and what helps you to transform it?
- Do you think there is a trade-off between living a happy life and a meaningful life?
- What emotions do you find most difficult when you reflect on your role as a leader and your desire to leave a mark on this world?

Exercises

- This week, notice your thoughts and the typical stories your mind keeps repeating (e.g. comments or beliefs about yourself, others, or the world). Write down your Top Five Tunes, give each of them a name.
- Pick one of your top tunes to sit with during your meditation and investigate your underlying beliefs and emotions as described above.
- During the day, take a few minutes to recognize if your present-moment experience is pleasant, unpleasant, or neutral. Pick different situations such as getting to work, having a conversation, waiting for something, or having a meal. What are your insights?
- If you have a habit that you would like to change, e.g. to drink less alcohol, eat less sugar, scroll less, watch fewer TV series, before you take that extra drink, cookie, press on the button,

take a moment to pause and breathe. Notice what emotions are present or ask yourself, *What am I unwilling to feel?* Then see if you can allow yourself to feel it. After 2-3 minutes, go ahead with what you wanted to do if you still would like to. Remember to do so with inner compassion.

- Pick a limiting belief that you feel is holding you back and go through the "Inquiry to Transform Limiting Beliefs" in the Going Deeper section.

WEEK 3–DAILY MEDITATION

MEDITATION ON THOUGHTS AND EMOTIONS

This week's meditation is designed to explore your thoughts and emotions. You can alternate this meditation with the Meditation on the Body from Week One.

Details about accessing this meditation can be found on my website.

https://www.susannevonderbecke.com/consciousimpact/meditation3

A transcript of this meditation can be found in the appendix.

WEEK 3–OPTIONAL BREATHWORK

BOX BREATHING

This breathing practice increases focus, concentration, and energy. It relieves stress and can be especially beneficial in high pressure moments, such as before a big presentation, or to reset your body and mind after a particularly stressful situation. Apparently, this is a breathing practice used by Navy SEALs. Before you start this simple breathing rhythm, it can be helpful to take a couple of deep breaths to relax your body.

1. Inhale through the nose for four counts, feeling your belly and ribs expand.
2. Hold your breath for a count of four.
3. Exhale through your mouth for a count of four counts, allowing your belly and ribs to return to their natural position.
4. Hold your breath for a count of four.

You can vary the pace of your counting, to find a rhythm that feels good for you. For example, if four seconds feel too long, count faster. To create harmony and signal predictability, the length of each inhalation, hold, exhalation, hold should be the same.

Repeat for several cycles as needed. Practice before your meditation or any time during the day.

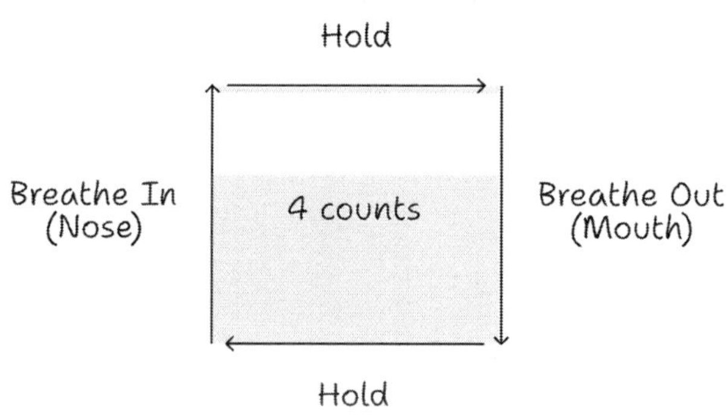

Chapter 8
Leading with Purpose
Chapter 3
Cultivating Presence & Awareness
Chapter 7
Cultivating an Open Heart
LEADERSHIP SKILLS
FOR CONSCIOUS IMPACT
Chapter 4
Sensing our Interbeing
Chapter 6
Being Comfortable with Discomfort
Chapter 5
Cultivating an Open Mind

CHAPTER 6

WEEK 4 | BEING COMFORTABLE WITH DISCOMFORT

"My comfort zone is like a little bubble around me, and I've pushed it in different directions and made it bigger and bigger until these objectives that seemed totally crazy eventually fall within the realm of the possible."

Alex Honold, Rock Climbing Athlete, Free Solo

Sometimes, a teacher or mentor says something that we think we understand, but it isn't until later that we grasp it on a deeper level. This happened to me when Tara Brach used the expression "go to the edge and soften."[73] I initially understood the part about life regularly bringing us to the edge, where things get uncomfortable, and how it is helpful to soften—stop clinging and resisting, relaxing the body, mind, and heart. What I only understood later is that we can make it our practice to *seek* the edge. When we seek the edge, we train our capacity to be with discomfort. This strengthens our ability to stay centered even during turmoil, find clarity in the chaos, and lead ourselves and others into the unknown future. But perhaps most importantly, it is at the edge where new possibilities arise. It is at the edge that new possibilities come into existence, propelling us forward by expanding our previous boundaries and integrating what was once thought impossible into our everyday experience.

As a business leader you are no stranger to challenges, complexities, and uncertainties. Most likely, you have already faced many situations of discomfort, arising from uncertainty, having your assumptions challenged, and stepping outside of your comfort zone by doing something new. Now we are asked, collectively, to perhaps face our biggest challenge yet: to redefine what it means to be human on this planet. We must find currently unimaginable ways to live as part of nature and build organizations and companies that contribute to the wellbeing of all people and living beings. We cannot lean back and wait for someone to invent that one silver-bullet technology that reverses climate change, restores biodiversity and ecosystems, facilitates social justice, and establishes peace on earth. While technology will play a role, relying on technology or someone else to fix this is an illusion created by our mind to keep us in the comfort zone of not having to change too much. It is impossible to change the world without changing ourselves.

By learning to embrace discomfort, we can transform it into a catalyst for growth, innovation, and transformation. We can learn to notice and even seek out discomfort to accelerate our inner growth, challenge our thinking, and reshape our perception of others and ourselves. This process frees us from the burden of the past and the assumption that, as leaders, we need to know everything. When we learn not just to endure discomfort but to relax into it, we can face difficult situations and rise to challenges with greater ease and a sense of flow.

The Unreal Others

One significant source of discomfort stems from our tendency to view others as fundamentally different from ourselves, often idealizing or demonizing them based on our conscious or unconscious assumptions about the world—the biases and patterns discussed earlier. Particularly when we are stressed or afraid, we fall back into the illusion of separation, creating distance between ourselves and others. And so, we create these *Unreal Others*, a term I first encountered through the teachings of Tara Brach. When we do that, we no longer see the other(s) as people, who have their own fears and dreams and try to find happiness, like us. Of course, we do that to other living beings too, often keeping animals in abhorrent conditions.

Some people become *unreal* simply because they don't matter to us. Sometimes, we are so self-absorbed that we don't see the vulnerability and inherent goodness of the person in front of us. This can be the cashier at the till, who we don't notice because our mind is somewhere else. Or it can be the man in Congo, mining cobalt for our clean energy transition in the most dire conditions, risking his life and barely making ends meet.[74]

Other times, we create Unreal Others of the people that actually mean a lot to us. I've heard stories of close friendships breaking apart over views about Donald Trump. During the COVID-19 pandemic some people reported big rifts inside their family over different opinions about vaccination. Recently, someone lost her best friend, for whom she is the godmother, over opposing views on the Israel-Palestine conflict. The world seems increasingly divided, and we go to great lengths to defend our positions.

I am not suggesting that we shouldn't take a stand and voice our beliefs. However, when we become convinced that we are right or superior to others, we lose our ability to keep an open mind and heart. We lose the connection within ourselves and become advocates for change from a place of separation and fear rather than connection and love. This approach only perpetuates the same problems that we are trying to solve.

In the worst cases, we dehumanize others to the extent that we no longer see them as people. How else could we justify going to war? How else could we collectively justify slavery, racism, or genocide?

As the climate crisis and other challenges continue to unfold, the world will likely become more divided. Populism is on the rise and international alliances are weakened. However, these existential challenges require a unified human response. Instead of more division we need global cooperation and must transcend our tendency to judge ourselves and others as either superior or inferior based on artificial distinctions of color, gender, political preference, or nationality. The work starts with us. We can make it a habit to notice when we create Unreal Others and use these moments to gain new perspectives. This could be paying attention to the cashier, looking into their eyes as we make the payment and for a moment sensing them as a real person. It could be the colleague at work who is late delivering on a target because his wife is sick (but we did not know). It could be the moment when you get mad for being stuck in traffic, until you suddenly realize that you *are* the traffic.

This happened to me during a retreat, where I, and more than a hundred other people, came to learn from the Tibetan teacher Lama Tsültrim Allione. I was looking forward to this rare opportunity to learn from such an esteemed teacher, deepen my meditation practice and spend four days in silence. Life had been so busy; my mind was restless and my body felt both charged and tired at the same time. But I had a hard time settling in.

The Dzogchen tradition uses a different meditation technique than the one I am trained in; there was much less silence than I had hoped for and more people than I had expected. During the first day and a half my mind would drive me crazy. It was continuously commenting on the situation and, to my surprise, on everyone around me. There was *me*, trying to find some inner peace, and there was *them*, the others. Each time I passed someone, my mind would come up with a whole story about who they were and what they might be thinking or feeling.

By the second day, I decided this had to stop. As my mind could not stop commenting on others, I decided to give it something else to focus on. Each time I passed another person, I silently repeated my wish for them and all beings to be well and free. In my mind, I would say: "may you feel loved, may you be happy." It worked. Not only did my mood improve with every person I encountered but, over time, the feeling of 'me vs. them' began to melt away. As my heart gradually opened, my mind calmed down, and I felt a greater sense of connection within myself and with everyone around me. I felt touched and grateful to see so many people from such diverse backgrounds, like me, taking time out of their busy schedules to reflect and learn from these ancient teachings.

Becoming aware of and unraveling what happens when we treat others as unreal, perhaps even unhuman, can unleash feelings of shame and guilt. The same is true when we realize that we have been othered, perhaps even believed in our inferiority and unworthiness. Being treated as an Unreal Other can leave inner scars for life. As mentioned earlier some of these are passed on over generations or manifest as collective trauma. As well as bringing loving awareness into these situations, forgiveness can play a big role in helping us shape a more humane future.

Forgiving Ourselves and Others

Even the word forgiveness can bring up a lot of resistance. So let me start by stressing that forgiving is not condoning. It does not mean that everyone is free to do any harm they want and then we all hold hands and say, "It's fine again" and move on. The forgiveness I am talking about requires radical responsibility, it requires the truth to be heard and the feelings to be felt. It is not an easy process but, in the end, we regain our sense of agency because the past can no longer determine our future.

Forgiveness is giving up all hope for a better past. It is the ultimate form of acceptance that allows us to move on with our lives, both individually and collectively. If we want to create a future that is based on a common understanding of interbeing and that serves the wellbeing of individuals, our community and nature, we must accept, process, and integrate our past.

In my experience, forgiveness cannot be rushed, it cannot be forced but it can be facilitated. We can create the individual and collective space that feels safe enough and large enough for forgiveness to take place.

Forgiveness also doesn't mean forgetting. In fact, it is a form of remembering. It is a remembering that allows us to free ourselves of the shackles of the Unreal Other, of seeing ourselves as either victim or perpetrator, and realizing that we are both. Investigating our lives, we all find situations in which we have been a victim of something, and situations where, intentionally or unintentionally, we have been a perpetrator. I presume you never killed someone, but can you honestly say that you don't know what anger, even rage is? Perhaps you have never been blinded by your desire and taken something that was not yours, but can you honestly say that you don't know craving, longing, or wanting? Have you never been deluded, caught in your own world unable to see the needs of the one in front of you? We all carry the seeds of destruction. And we all carry the seeds of love and compassion. In fact, the latter is our nature. As you may have experienced in your meditation, our inherent nature of being is loving and benevolent. But we keep forgetting and our view gets clouded by our thinking and attachment.

Surely, you might say, there are limits to forgiveness: some acts are simply unforgivable! And I would agree. If I just imagine someone seriously harming my family, I know I cannot guarantee anything. Some injustices make me so furious I can totally see myself taking revenge rather than even contemplating forgiveness! But others have done it in the most unthinkable circumstances.

When my husband came back from an impact conference in Rwanda, he told me about his visit to the memorial of the Rwandan genocide, the brutal mass murder of over half a million Tutsis and moderate Hutus which occurred in the country in 1994. At the memorial was a woman, who was sharing her story and telling the audience about the war. She was a survivor. She had witnessed the murder of her husband, and three of her four children were killed. I felt my heart trembling with sadness. My husband continued, "And right next to her was sitting a man. This man was the murderer of her husband and children."

"What?!" I exclaimed, sitting up completely straight and ready to pounce. "How is that even possible?"

"Forgiveness," he said. "The woman told us about how she freed her heart and the burden she was carrying through forgiveness."

I was silent. My husband continued. "We also heard the man's story, the murderer. He told us how he went to prison and how he was sure he was going to die there, expecting that people would take revenge. But they did not. And this opened a new possibility, where he could come back into the village where he and his victims had all lived together in one community before the genocide, after serving his sentence, and start anew."

When you look into the history of this conflict, it quickly becomes clear that, as with so many conflicts in Africa or the Middle East, European colonization, white superiority thinking, and arbitrary categorization of humans played a huge role in the unfolding tragedy. Seeing how 'my people,' the Europeans—and as a German, a country that started two world wars and committed the largest genocide in history—have contributed to so much suffering in the world makes me feel responsible. Considering how we in the 'Global North' play a major part in causing the degradation of our planet and the unfolding environmental and human suffering also makes me feel responsible. These thoughts are always followed by, *Well, but it wasn't me*, or *Those perpetrators were not my people*, or *It is not my fault*. And that is also true.

I don't know what it would take to establish some kind of planetary reconciliation, for both victims and perpetrators to be heard and at the same time allow us to move beyond identifying as one or the other. But what I do know is that we can begin with ourselves. That we are likely to perpetuate the pain that our ancestors experienced if we don't turn toward it. Many of our parents and ancestors did not have the ability to do the inner work as we can. Many of them were caught up in war, poverty, and oppressive political regimes. If you, like me, live in relative peace and prosperity then we might both have much easier conditions to do our inner work to facilitate healing. Perhaps that is our responsibility.

Embracing the Don't Know Mind

I used to think the edge is at the far end of a spectrum. But sometimes, the edge is right in the middle. The extreme side of an argument that is diametrically opposed to our own opinion does not (usually) make us uncomfortable, but rather it is the space in between that we must cross. It is the possibility that two seemingly contradictory perspectives can be equally true. But it is in that space that new thinking can emerge and solutions be found.

Christiana Figueres is a Costa Rican diplomat renowned for her pivotal role in negotiating the Paris Agreement, a landmark international treaty on climate change adopted in 2015. Appointed as the Executive Secretary of the UN Framework Convention on Climate Change in 2010, she took charge after the unsuccessful Copenhagen Climate Conference and faced the daunting task of revitalizing global climate negotiations. After being asked in a press conference if she believed that a global agreement would ever be possible, and spontaneously blurting out, "Not in my lifetime," she realized that the first thing she had to do was change her mindset.[75]

Christiana Figueres has repeatedly credited her meditation practice and the teachings of Zen master Thích Nhất Hạnh for helping her overcome a deep personal crisis and giving her skills that enabled the successful adoption, in 2015, of the Paris Agreement by 196 countries. Her mindfulness practice helped her stay grounded amid difficult conversations. She managed to accomplish a seemingly impossible mission by changing her own mindset to what she refers to as stubborn optimism, incorporating deep listening, and moving beyond the simplistic view of countries as either victims or perpetrators.

> *"Early on in our path toward the Paris Agreement we understood that our work to bring all countries to common ground was best served by suspending judgment and devoting ourselves to listening deeply to every participant to understand their respective needs and wants. It was through that deep listening that we were able to let collective solutions emerge at the right time and recognize the seeds that needed to be watered in order to blossom into fruition. Finally, we were blessed to know that, ultimately, we are all interconnected with one another and with all other living beings, and it is this interconnection that guides our path forward."*[76]

Being able to listen to different perspectives, suspending judgment and staying at the edge of discomfort right in the middle of different perspectives allowed new solutions to emerge. The psychologist Carl Jung regarded "holding the tension of opposites" as essential in achieving a higher level of psychological integration and wholeness.

Holding contradictory perspectives, staying with the feeling of 'not knowing' and not judging, not forcing a decision until it emerges, requires a high level of awareness and the ability to relax into discomfort. As we start to relax physically and mentally, we stop grasping or rejecting one view over another and create the inner spaciousness from which new perspectives can emerge. We need those perspectives. Our old way of thinking in terms of Good vs. Bad, Left-wing vs. Right-wing, Communism vs. Capitalism, Market vs. State, Owners vs. Employees, etc., are no longer serving us. Our debates are moving in circles and the divisions between the camps are widening. My impression is that most people don't identify with either side, but they feel they have to choose. However, for most of us, developing and formulating balanced views that take account of shades of light and dark, rather than stark black or white, is much more difficult. At least it is for me. Quite to the exasperation of my husband, who is generally very nuanced in his perspective, I can take great joy from arguing in bold black and white capital letters! As Christiana Figueres and Tom Rivett-Carnac wrote in *The Future We Choose*, "Paradoxically, systemic change is a deeply personal endeavor. Our social and economic structures are a product of our way of thinking."[77]

As leaders, we often feel pressured to have all the answers, but admitting that we don't know something can be incredibly liberating. Embracing the 'Don't Know Mind' encourages curiosity, open-mindedness, and a willingness to explore new possibilities without the burden of preconceived notions. This mindset fosters an environment where questioning and learning are valued over simply having the right answers, leading to more innovative and effective solutions.

Julia is a senior sustainability advisor and gets hired by companies to advise them on their CSR strategy and how to comply with an increasingly long list of EU regulations. "At first," she explains, "I saw myself as an activist in a suit, stepping into boardrooms and telling them to wake up." But she quickly realized that this *Me vs. Them* perspective was not working. Instead, she had to become her clients' Critical Friend, to understand their perspectives and help them along the way. When we talked about embracing a 'Don't Know Mind' and getting comfortable with not always knowing the right solution, she sighed with relief. "I am so tired of thinking I need to be the one who knows it all." She said the best client relationships are the ones where there is enough trust to acknowledge what she knows and what she doesn't. "There are so many moving pieces, new technologies that will be built and we have no idea yet how much they will cost." Net-zero emissions is the target but the path to get there is only emerging step by step.

As 'experts' and as leaders we often feel that we should have all the answers. It takes courage to say that we don't know. We become vulnerable to not being respected as an expert or perceived as unprofessional. However, perhaps the best leaders today are the ones who, at the right moment, can step aside, move beyond their ego, and let solutions emerge from the tension of opposites.

Leading into the Unknown

We generally experience the Unknown as stressful. Our brains are wired to keep us safe and consequently prefer certainty over uncertainty because uncertainty means we could get hurt, we might fail, be ridiculed, dismissed or whatever your fear is. However, there is a particular aliveness, a sense of emergence in the Unknown that steers us from a place of disconnection to connection. As Brené Brown explains:

> *"I spent a lot of years trying to outrun or outsmart vulnerability by making things certain and definite, black and white, good and bad. My inability to lean into the discomfort of vulnerability limited the fullness of those important experiences that are wrought with uncertainty: Love, belonging, trust, joy, and creativity to name a few."*[78]

The Unknown is our emerging future, it is something that is not yet born; it is empty, without form. In our Western thinking we often mistake emptiness for *nothingness*, whereas the better description would be *full of potentiality*. When we meditate and our mind becomes still, even if just for a moment, we can glimpse this full potentiality. Its quality is light, expansive, and benevolent. (If you have not yet experienced it, don't worry. Keep going, you are not doing it wrong, it just takes time—and consistency.)

The futurist and early environmentalist Buckminster Fuller once said, "You never change things by fighting the existing reality. To change something, build a model that makes the existing model obsolete." Building new models requires us to lead ourselves and others into the Unknown, and who better to do this than business leaders and entrepreneurs?

Diego De Nicola, a philosopher, performance coach, and entrepreneur, believes we need a new model for how we teach our children. The current school system in Switzerland, as well as in many countries across the world, is highly standardized, with uniform classes for all children and 45-minute teaching units—long enough to make children listen but short enough to discourage too many questions. This system does not accommodate the individual needs and talents of children who may excel quickly in some subjects and need more time in others. Uniform arrival times don't match everyone's optimal learning periods, and the standard holiday schedules are inconvenient for many parents.

Initially, De Nicola approached school directors and other officials with his ideas but found no success. Undeterred, he founded a new school that offers flexible arrival and departure times, operates four days a week (with an optional fifth day), and allows holidays to be taken when it suits working parents. In an era where knowledge is readily accessible via the internet, children at this school engage in question-driven learning guided by a team of educators, mentors, and experts. Now in its fourth year, the school is recognized by Swiss authorities and its classes are fully enrolled. Reflecting on the journey, De Nicola said, "We had no idea if this was going to work. When we opened, we had six children—and three of them were mine."

Sometimes, we need to venture into the Unknown to create something entirely new. Embracing uncertainty can be our ally, as it makes anything possible. The beginning of something new always involves the ending of something else that we must let go of.

Ryan Gellert, CEO of the outdoor clothing company Patagonia, expressed this sentiment in an interview: "I want us... taking responsibility for [our] product and ultimately create as closed of a loop as possible for the materials that we use. In doing that, there is a point where we're probably starting to cannibalize new product sales with second-hand [sales], and that's a problem I embrace."

Trusting the Process

Trusting the process doesn't mean sitting passively on the sofa or a meditation cushion. It means stopping the frantic chase for a desired outcome and instead making room for possibilities to emerge, both internally and externally. It means finding our way back when we feel lost in the unknown, remembering that we are part of something bigger, that our actions matter, and that whatever happens next is a co-creation with others and follows its own timing. This approach allows us not only to get comfortable with uncertainty but to relax into it and thrive within it.

As leaders who aim to create a positive impact, we are acutely aware that our window of time to fix things is getting smaller, and our own lifetimes are limited. We want results, and we want them now. When something isn't working, we often blame someone and rush to fix it. But how has this approach worked for you so far? How do you feel when you lead your life and others from this place? Is it preventing you from experiencing a sense of ease, satisfaction, or even joy in your work?

One of my other dear teachers, Lama Tilmann Lhündrup, once instructed us to "try our absolute hardest to relax as much as possible." We all started to laugh, it seemed impossible! But it is just one of these tensions of opposites. On the meditation cushion, it means that we aim to be fully alert and completely relaxed, without grasping or rejecting what happens inside of us. In life, it means that we are fully aware of what is happening around and inside of us, sense what is our part to do, and choose the best possible response. With practice, we don't waste so much time or life energy on resisting reality, anymore. Instead, we experience a greater sense of ease, flow, and wonder, moving from experiencing Life as something that we need to control and manage (*It is my responsibility to make it happen*) to Life is happening through us (*I am co-creating life as it arises in the present moment.*)[79]

Having a vision of what we want to achieve is important, but ironically, what will help us get there is letting it go. Not letting it go in the sense that we don't care anymore but in the sense that we can trust in the emergence of solutions when the time is right. Trusting the process helps us to loosen our grip on needing to control everything (which is an impossible endeavor anyway) and surrender and find a way to be able to relax into the discomfort.

In my experience, people have different ways of finding that trust and different words to describe it. For Christiana Figueres, 'stubborn optimism' is her inspiration to keep going despite challenges:

> *"Optimism is not about blindly ignoring the realities that surround us, that's foolishness. It's also not a naïve faith that everything will take care of itself, even if we do nothing. That is irresponsibility. The optimism I'm speaking of is not the result of an achievement, it is the necessary input to meeting a challenge. It is, in fact, the only way to increase our chance of success."* [80]

Perhaps you too have been asked if you are an optimist or a pessimist. I never know what to answer. My husband seems to be a true optimist. He always sees the best in people and emphasizes all the progress we have made as humans. I see people and I feel their pain, their confusion, their sadness. And at the same time, I see so much goodness in them. I look at humanity and see so much destruction and so much beauty. I know that without mud there is no lotus, and I think there is a real possibility for humanity to create a beautiful new chapter for all of us. I don't think it is just going to happen, I think we have to do our part. I am, it turns out, a possibilist.[81]

Another word, apart from optimism or possibilism, that may help you trust in the process is *hope*. As the renowned environmental activist Jane Goodall writes "Hope is often misunderstood. People tend to think that it is simply passive wishful thinking: I hope something will happen but I'm not going to do anything about it. This is indeed the opposite of real hope, which requires action and engagement."[82] The need to detach ourselves from the desired outcome resonates in the Czech statesman and author Václav Havel's description: "Hope is not the conviction that something will turn out well but the certainty that something makes sense, regardless of how it turns out."

Trusting the process will help you find a sense of ease with discomfort and accept challenges as integral parts of your growth journey. When I get lost in uncertainty and I lose my trust, I go into nature and I meditate. Being in nature reconnects me with a sense of awe. The inherent intelligence, that is so much more than my mind could ever grasp, is so obvious to me that I find it easier to be ok with not knowing. Similarly, when I meditate and I can connect to the stillness in between my thoughts, I feel the inherently expansive and benevolent quality of our awareness and I remember that I can trust in that. As we become more comfortable with discomfort, we start to experience a sense of flow and even joy in the midst of difficulty. With equanimity—one of the four wholesome states that we will explore next week—we become more centered and open, enabling us to co-create with life as it unfolds.

Week 4–Going Deeper: Working with Forgiveness

Working with forgiveness can be a powerful way to accelerate our inner healing, to practice radical acceptance of a past that we cannot change in order to create a future with greater freedom, ease, and connection.

There are two ways you can work with this.

1. You can work with forgiveness generally and make it a regular practice to help you let go. Read the phrases either silently or out loud. Repeat a few times and pay attention to your emotions and the sensations in your body. Allow yourself to feel and open your mind. Don't judge your experience; stay open with a kind and loving attention. This practice of forgiveness can free us from blame, and be a powerful reminder of our interbeing and the common human experience of human suffering.

2. You can work with forgiveness specifically. Perhaps there is a particular event that you have not been able to move on from, where you feel now is the right time to bring in more spaciousness through forgiveness. Bring the situation to mind and ask yourself what type of forgiveness is needed here? Whether we want to forgive someone who hurt us or ask for forgiveness for hurting someone else, we usually need to also forgive ourselves. For some of us, this is the hardest and most necessary thing to do.

Note that if you find that you are not yet ready to forgive someone or yourself, you can use these phases instead: *May I forgive them / myself, when I am ready*. Be patient and gentle with yourself. If you feel overwhelmed during this exercise, return to your breath by gently inhaling through the nose and slowly exhaling through the mouth.

Reconnecting with nature and practicing the loving-kindness meditation in Week Five can also be helpful.

The following phrases are from Jack Kornfield, with my own explanations and little tweaks based on my own practice.[83]

Asking for forgiveness from others

There are many ways that I have hurt and harmed others, have betrayed or abandoned them, caused them suffering knowingly or unknowingly, out of my pain, fear, anger, and confusion.

Repeat the sentence a few times. If you work with a specific person in mind, visualize them in front of you. As you see the person in front of you, imagine how you made them feel and acknowledge the pain you caused them. Notice any emotions and sensations arising. Breathe and hold your experience with compassion. Finally, you can say:

I ask for your forgiveness. / May you forgive me.

Forgiving yourself

There are many ways that I have hurt and harmed myself. I have betrayed or abandoned myself many times through thought, word, or deed, knowingly or unknowingly.

Repeat the sentence a few times. If you work with a specific situation in mind, where you hurt someone or let yourself get hurt, connect with the memory of this situation for as long as it feels safe for you to do so. Notice any arising emotions and sensations and hold your experience with compassion. It can be helpful to acknowledge the confusion and pain you were carrying at the time. Perhaps you can see your younger self and give them the compassion and understanding that you would have needed then. Feel the goodness of your own heart.

Breathe. Finally, you can say:

I forgive myself. / May I forgive myself.

Forgiving others

> *There are many ways that I have been harmed by others, abused or abandoned, knowingly or unknowingly, in thought, word, or deed.*

Repeat the sentence a few times. If you work with a specific situation in mind, connect with the memory of this situation for as long as it feels safe for you to do so. Notice any arising emotions and sensations and hold your experience with compassion. If it gets too much, look up and connect with something beautiful. You can always come back to this. If it feels right, continue. See the person in front of you. Sense their delusion and the pain that caused them to react in the way they did. Perhaps you know, or can sense, part of their story. If this feels right to you, you can imagine them as a child, reminding you of their inherent goodness, just like yours. And when you are ready you can say to them:

> *I now remember the many ways others have hurt me, wounded me out of fear, pain, confusion, and anger. I have carried this pain in my heart for too long. To the extent that I am ready, I offer them forgiveness. To those who have caused me harm, I offer my forgiveness, I forgive you. / May I forgive you.*

Week 4–Questions and Exercises

Questions

- How does 'othering' show up in your life? Consider your family, work environment, community, and culture.
- Should Nature be recognized as a living entity with its own legal rights to protect it from harm? Do we treat Nature as an Unreal Other?
- Are there people in your life that, if you could, you would like to ask for forgiveness?
- What would you need to be able to forgive yourself or to seek forgiveness in a situation where you created an Unreal Other?
- How important is it for your identity as a leader to know what to do?
- What does "trusting the process" mean to you? How does it apply to your current situation in your personal life, at work and to your role as a changemaker?
- What helps you to find trust in challenging and highly uncertain situations?

Exercises

- Notice when you are treating others as 'unreal', how does that feel in your body?
- What are the moments that you are most likely to treat others as 'unreal'?
- If you feel called to work with forgiveness, go through the exercise in the Going Deeper section of this chapter.
- Find opposing views that are both true for you. Write them down, connecting them through AND, notice if there is a shift. (For example: *I feel responsible, and it is not my fault*, or *I should be more accepting of myself and there are so many areas where I could be a better human being.*) Notice if you feel different.

Week 4–Daily Meditation

Meditation on the Breath

This week's meditation is designed to experience an inner spaciousness.

Details about accessing this meditation can be found on my website.

https://www.susannevonderbecke.com/consciousimpact/meditation4

A transcript of this meditation can be found in the appendix.

You can alternate this meditation with the previous meditations according to what practice you want to deepen. For grounding and resting in the present moment use *Meditation on the Body*, to deepen your sense of interconnectedness the *Meditation on Interbeing*, to become more aware of your thinking use *Meditation on Thoughts and Emotions.*

Week 4–Optional Breathwork

4–7–8 Breath

This simple breathing practice can quickly calm down your body by making your exhalation longer than your inhalation and thereby activating your Parasympathetic Nervous System. It is an effective tool when you feel stressed, anxious, or are having difficulties falling asleep. You can do this practice standing, sitting, or lying down.

1. Inhale through your nose for a count of four.
2. Hold your breath for a count of seven. (If this feels too long and you are running out of air, make it shorter, don't force it.)
3. Exhale through your mouth with pursed lips for a count of eight.

Repeat for four cycles or continue for as long as it feels beneficial. Use this practice as needed.

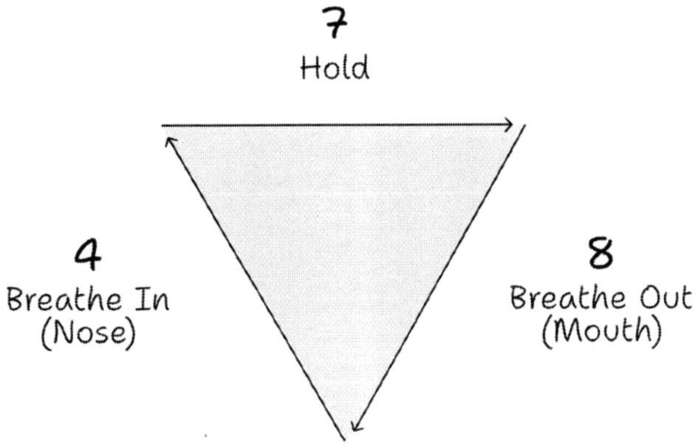

RECONNECTING ON THE LEVEL OF THE HEART

After spending the last two weeks exploring your mind to better understand how your thoughts and emotions influence your behavior, we will now turn toward reconnecting with your heart. Ultimately, our practice boils down to this: as our mind becomes more still and we become less identified with our mind, we can more easily listen to the wisdom of our heart. Cultivating the qualities of kindness, compassion, joy and equanimity strengthens our capacity as changemakers to address the problems in this world without getting burned out. With an open heart we can see and feel the beauty in this world, which in turn makes it easier to also let ourselves be touched by the pain in this world. Consequently, we become more fully alive and in love with the world while also becoming more resilient. Your heart will also guide you on your journey of leading with purpose. When we let ourselves be guided by the heart, we find meaning in creating wellbeing for ourselves and the world around us. Our heart reconnects us with the values that matter to us and guides us as we lead our organizations into a new future. While our mind understands the urgency of the problems we face, our heart reminds us to become the change we want to see without taking ourselves too seriously.

Chapter 8
Leading with Purpose
Chapter 3
Cultivating Presence & Awareness
Chapter 7
Cultivating an Open Heart
LEADERSHIP SKILLS
FOR CONSCIOUS IMPACT
Chapter 4
Sensing our Interbeing
Chapter 6
Being Comfortable with Discomfort
Chapter 5
Cultivating an Open Mind

CHAPTER 7

WEEK 5 | CULTIVATING AN OPEN HEART

"The mind creates the abyss, and the heart crosses it."
Sri Nisargadatta

Not long ago I was invited to a dinner. I did not know many people there and after a short time I found myself in a conversation with a very friendly person, who had just recently moved to that town. I asked him what made him move into this part of the world and, with a big smile, he answered, "My wife." He explained, "You know, my wife is this mathematical genius, she studied at one of the best technical universities in France, worked in Silicon Valley and now she is one of the youngest members of the executive team at the company she works at." I smiled. I love it when men are proud of their partner's work and supportive of their careers. "That's great," I said, "and what does the company do?"

"They are in robotics, in intelligence," he answered. I had a hard time picturing what that meant and, as if he sensed my wondering, he added confidently, "They are specialized in building the most advanced defense technologies." Now there were even more question marks popping up above my head. After a few seconds of silence, I blurted out, "You mean," I paused, "weapons?" Sensing my surprise and bewilderment, for a second he looked a bit uncomfortable. (Never invite me for a dinner party, I am terrible at small talk.) But it did not take long for him to regain his composure and he started to explain.

"You know, they are only selling it to democratic countries. And it is only for defending our democratic values."

"Hmm," I said, wondering if he would like to engage in a longer discussion about that or if it was better to see if dinner was ready.

I know that the idea that humanity simply decides to stop producing and destroying all existing weapons is completely idealistic and does not do justice to the complexity of geopolitics. Or is it? But that's not the point of the story. When this friendly man was talking about his wife, he sounded confident, authentic; I could sense how much he loved her. However, when I asked him if the company was producing weapons, he responded with a well-rehearsed sentence about democracy that felt much less authentic. It seemed that he was no longer answering from his heart but that he was telling himself a story, rationalized in his mind, and his heart was somewhere else.

I cannot possibly know what he was truly thinking or feeling. My interpretation may well be just a mirroring of my own discomfort with the weapons industry. But the reason I am sharing this is that I think we all know that feeling when our mind tries to convince us of something, and we want to believe it, and yet, a nagging sensation in our hearts tells us that something is not right. Have you ever been in this situation? So many times, I've heard people's regrets after failing to follow their hearts. They felt, somehow, they were heading in the wrong direction but they did not dare to listen to their hearts because their mind was telling them a different story.

The thing is, our hearts are wise. Our brains are brilliant at helping us create the world we want, while our hearts are brilliant at helping us create the world we need. As discussed in previous chapters, the stories we tell ourselves about ourselves, others and how the world works can give rise to cruelty and violence that feels like staring into the abyss. However, when our mind is lost in the illusion of separation, our heart reminds us of our common humanity and shows us the way forward.

However, listening to our hearts can feel like a very risky endeavor. Just the idea of leading with an open heart reminds me of open-heart surgery and evokes a sensation of extreme vulnerability. Considering the cut-throat dynamics at the top of our corporations or in politics, you might think leading with an open heart would be suicidal. People would last a few months before they'd be eaten alive by their competitors and critics. It is true, there are many situations where speaking and acting from the heart takes courage: it is risky because we can get hurt when others do not agree with us. We might even feel embarrassed listening to our heart because listening to our mind and 'really thinking things through' is regarded as the most sane thing to do. But leading from the heart does not mean that you shut off your brain.

In the Western world in particular, it seems that we place so much importance on the rational and intellectual capabilities of our minds, to the extent that our highest wish is to be identified as excelling in rationality and intellectualism, that often we discount the movements in our hearts as something sentimental and quite irrelevant to solving the problems we face. The reality could not be further from the truth. When our minds and hearts are not aligned, we seem to create more problems than solutions. It is even possible to physically measure our brain and heart coherence. When our heart is in alignment with our thoughts and emotions, our bodies enter a healthy, high-performance state of optimal organ functioning, and we experience less stress and more mental clarity.[84]

Some other cultures do not make a distinction between mind and heart. For example, in the Chinese language the character for *heart* also refers to meanings related to the mind. In Vedantic philosophy, the heart is often referred to as the seat of the soul (*Atman*) and the center of consciousness. The ancient Greek philosopher Aristotle believed the heart to be the center of the body's vital functions, as well as of our thoughts and emotions.

From a mindfulness perspective, our heart and mind are also interconnected. While one part of the practice focuses on stabilizing the mind and developing insight, it would be incomplete without the cultivation of wholesome states of mind, which can also be described as qualities of the heart.[85] These qualities, called the four Brahmaviharas, also known as the 'Four Divine Abodes' are the focus of this chapter: Loving-Kindness, or universal goodwill (*Mettā*), Compassion (*Karunā*), Joy *(Muditā*) and Equanimity (*Upekkhā*). Cultivating these wholesome states of mind (or heart) has proven to be incredibly impactful in shifting our way of being and thinking from a place of disconnection (separation and fear) to connection (interbeing and love). Many times, I have heard how these practices helped people to shine a light when they felt stuck and helpless. For me, they have certainly shifted the baseline of my happiness.

All four qualities are inherently connected, as Jack Kornfield explains beautifully in *The Wise Heart*: "When consciousness is peaceful and open, we rest in equanimity. As our peaceful heart meets other beings, it fills with love. When this love meets pain, it transforms itself naturally into compassion. And when this same open-hearted love meets happiness, it becomes joy. In this way, the radiant abodes spontaneously reflect and connect the whole world."[86]

The Power of Kindness

Kindness is the medicine of our times. It reminds us who we really are. A video of a soccer match circulated on LinkedIn; I don't normally follow sports much, but this post captured my attention. It was the closing ceremony of the UEFA Super Cup and the players lined up to shake hands with the officials and collect their medal. At the far end of the line stood the UEFA President Alexander Ceferin. Between the president and another official stood a young girl, an invited fan, visually impaired. She waited patiently as several players passed by without noticing her. They greeted and shook hands with the officials, over her head, before moving on to collect their medals. But one of the players, Jack Grealish, stopped and talked to her. He showed her kindness. Even when the UEFA president tapped him on the arm, asking him to keep the queue moving, Grealish took his time to talk to the little fan. People in the stadium started clapping, Jack Grealish made headlines in the papers next morning, and video clips of the scene went viral on social media.[87]

We are starved of kindness. There is something about kindness in our highly competitive and transactional world that warms our hearts and reminds us of our common humanity. Loving-kindness is our antidote to Othering. Although our human history is full of violence and destruction, it is also full of kindness. There is plenty of evidence from anthropology, psychology and history that humans are inherently good and driven by a natural tendency toward cooperation and kindness.[88]

Kindness is our antidote to a perfectionism that does not allow us to make mistakes and that fosters the feeling of never being quite good enough. Kindness reminds us of our inherent goodness, both within ourselves and others. Take a moment to think of your strongest relationships. Is it possible that these are the ones that make you feel worthy and loved, independent of your performance or behavior? Our best friends are often the ones that see our goodness, even when we may have forgotten it. Unconditional friendship allows us to learn, grow, and make mistakes and it motivates us to get up again.

Loving-kindness is our true nature. It is not something we need to develop; it is something that we need only to allow to shine through. As the poet Rumi wrote: "Your task is not to seek for love, but merely to seek and find all the barriers within yourself that you have built against it." When your mind starts to settle and you are able to rest, more and more, in awareness itself, you can experience this inherent goodwill. At the beginning it might be just glimpses in between thoughts that are naturally coming and going. Over time, as you befriend your monkey mind and stop clinging to your thoughts and emotions, you can sense the inherently spacious, expansive, empty (in the sense of being *full of potential*) and benevolent nature of your being.

Sometimes, sensing our inherent goodness seems like a big stretch and the tale of the two wolves, often attributed to an indigenous American parable, describes much better our everyday experience. In this story, an elder Cherokee is teaching his grandson about life. "A fight is raging inside me," he said to the boy. "It is a terrible fight between two wolves. One is evil—he is anger, envy, sorrow, regret, greed, arrogance, self-pity, guilt, resentment, inferiority, lies, false pride, superiority and ego. The other stands for joy, peace, love, hope, sharing, serenity, humility, kindness, benevolence, friendship, empathy, generosity, truth, compassion and faith. The same fight is going on inside you and inside every other person, too." His grandson thought about it for a minute and then asked his grandfather, "Which wolf will win?" The old Cherokee simply replied, "The one you feed."

This tale serves as a reminder that we have a choice: We can choose to cultivate what is wholesome or what is destructive. We can literally rewire our brains through the deliberate practice of nourishing the good in our lives. Moreover, I believe there is another teaching here. What if we realized that this so-called Evil Wolf is just afraid, tired, hungry or hurt? What would happen if we tended to it with kindness and patience and made it feel safe and loved?

My experience is that we are often afraid of this wolf inside us. We fear that if others discover our anger, envy, greed, self-pity, etc., we will be deemed unlovable. We fall short of our own expectations and cut ourselves off from seeing our inherent goodness. But as you've probably discovered, you are not perfect, at least not in the way you think you should be. Nobody is. However, through the power of kindness, we can transform how we relate to ourselves. It allows us to hold all our weirdness, conditioning, scars and pain in a caring way. Kindness is fundamentally healing, as it sees both our brokenness and our wholeness. When we let our hearts be filled with loving-kindness, it automatically spills over to others, strengthening our relationships and the invisible ties all around us. With loving-kindness, we can make room for our individuality and uniqueness as well as our common humanity. Making the deliberate choice to bring more kindness into our lives reconnects us both with ourselves and with the world around us.

Compassion Means Action

As described above, when our mind becomes peaceful, we can experience the loving quality of our heart, expressed as goodwill toward all living beings. When this heart meets suffering, compassion arises. The quality of kindness reflects our wish for all beings to be happy and compassion reflects our wish for all beings to be without suffering.

While *empathy* generally refers to our ability to take the perspective and feel the emotions of another person, *compassion* includes a strong desire to help and reduce the suffering. In that sense, compassion is all about action. It finds its expression in our active participation to reduce suffering. Unlike an irrational and sentimental emotion, compassion is our natural instinct. Humans depend on empathy and compassion for their survival like no other species.

Compared to other animals, human babies are helpless for quite a long time. Little baby chimpanzees can eat by themselves, humans can't. Our babies can't sit up straight, let alone run away from danger. Compared to other animals, our babies are born premature and, as the only animal without fur, claws, sharp teeth or wings, we are quite vulnerable out in the wild. Therefore, we needed to form communities to survive. Whilst not being the only mammals to demonstrate empathy and compassion, our human brain has developed, relatively, many more neurons and neural circuits to feel what other beings feel (empathy) and to care about other beings' suffering (compassion). According to Dacher Keltner, Professor of Psychology at the University of California, Berkeley, "We became the super caregiving species, to the point where acts of care improve our physical health and lengthen our lives."[89] Although the 'survival of the fittest' theory, popularly attributed to Charles Darwin, is often used to justify our human selfishness and competitive nature, in fact, Darwin found that "sympathy is our strongest instinct, sometimes stronger than self-interest" and that "the most sympathetic members would flourish best, and rear the greatest number of offspring."[90]

I was born with a lot of compassion, but it certainly did not feel like a competitive advantage. In the Introduction, I shared with you my personal journey and how from an early age seeing the suffering of others in the news would evoke a strong wish to do something about it. But not knowing what to do and also not being able to do much was quite painful. Often when I hear people talk about our current crises, pictures of people and animals affected by floods and heatwaves, victims of the atrocities of war, I hear them say: "I am not watching the news anymore. I care, I really do. But I just can't take it." And I get it, it hurts. Several years ago, when I first started studying mindfulness meditation more deeply, I confronted my teacher Lama Ingrid about that. "Compassion doesn't make me feel good. It makes me feel sad and weak. I don't see how that is helping me." She looked at me with a smile and said: "You are lacking wisdom." What sounded like an insult, delivered with a loving smile, was actually a fundamental lesson in mindfulness.

Mindfulness has two wings: compassion and wisdom. With only one wing, we cannot fly. Wisdom is our deeper understanding of the bigger picture; that suffering is part of life, that everything is temporary, awareness of yourself and the world, and the ability to hold it all with a sense of peace and loving presence. As effective leaders of change, we must strengthen both wings of mindfulness. If we only feel the suffering in this world but don't understand that everything is impermanent and interconnected, our hearts will crumble, and we will burn out. Perhaps you have already experienced this. Remembering that everything is continuously changing and that we are part of a greater whole can help us bear the pain and not take our suffering too personally. But we also need the other wing: compassion. Compassion fuels our desire to make things better and helps us to become love in action.

At least once a year, I try to go on a retreat to deepen my meditation practice and dedicate time for insight and regeneration. One November, when the days were getting shorter and darker, I was on my way to the retreat. I was exhausted, my body felt tired, and my mind was foggy. I got off at the wrong train station in the dark. In the café, as I waited for the next train, I made myself tea, opened the little pot of milk and poured the milk into the trash bin instead of my cup. At that moment, I realized that I was probably close to burnout. "But how could that happen?" I asked myself. Even throughout the busyness of the year, I had managed to keep up my mindfulness practice, and meditated almost every day. Should this not have helped me to refuel or at least notice where I was heading? Then, in the meditation hall, Lama Tilmann Lhündrup started guiding us into the first meditation, and tears started rolling down my face. All of a sudden, I knew why. I had forgotten the key ingredient: compassion! Without compassion and loving-kindness, our meditation and mindfulness practice becomes dry. I had powered through the year, in many ways driven by the desire to create a positive impact, and nearly every day I had sat on the meditation cushion, acknowledging my restlessness and tiredness, just as I taught you in the previous chapter, but I had forgotten the most important thing: to receive the present moment with kindness and compassion.

Self-compassion is a tricky thing for many of us. Possibly *inner compassion* may be a more helpful label for you. It is interesting why, in our otherwise self-absorbed society, inner compassion is so difficult. Business leaders, in particular, tell me that they are afraid to lose their 'edge'. That they are afraid to get too soft on themselves and so start slacking and not perform at their best anymore. But I've never seen that happen. In contrast, when we think we need more discipline, often what we really need is more compassion. Compassion is an act of courage because rather than running away from our suffering we turn toward it. Compassion seeks to alleviate suffering not by ignoring it but by transforming it. Sometimes, this transformation occurs simply by tending to our wounds from a place of love rather than fear, which then enables us to make more wholesome choices.

Another objection to self-compassion that I hear a lot is that we think our suffering does not count. Especially for leaders who are aware of the problems in our world—people are dying of hunger, leaving their homes in search of safety, risking their lives, etc.—our own everyday kind of suffering can seem unimportant. Sometimes, when it seems to me that I get stressed for nothing—because the kids are fighting, my husband said something, I don't have time, I still need to organize this, and remember to buy that, and it is all so bloody annoying—I get angry with my suffering. I call it my "bourgeois suffering," the suffering from having the privilege to have a good life. But then I remember to meet even this bourgeois suffering with compassion and make it my practice to open into the discomfort, let go of my judgment and reconnect with my heart.

The awareness that there are other people who suffer much more and are in truly bad situations is usually not helpful in transforming our present-moment experience. If others suffer more, it does not mean that we suffer less. It means we probably have much better conditions to do our inner work and therefore have a responsibility to do something about it. We can use situations of small pain as our practice to become more resilient and strengthen our capacity to deal with big pain when it arises. Each one of us, no matter how privileged and lucky, will experience the big pains of losing loved ones, of sickness, aging and death.

With compassion we can tend to the world and to ourselves. As we build our capacity to turn toward the pain in the world, we must also include ourselves. Experiencing our interbeing with others and with

Nature, our commitment to alleviate our own suffering ripples out in ever widening circles and can bring healing for ourselves and this planet. On this journey, we slowly free ourselves from our own entanglements while also being able to hold our suffering with more lightness and connect to a deep sense of joy, the joy of being alive.

Bringing Back the Joy

The third wholesome quality we can cultivate is joy, in particular sympathetic joy. Sympathetic joy comes from taking pleasure in other people's wellbeing and therefore gives infinite opportunities to experience joy, even when we might be going through difficult times ourselves. Cultivating joy is incredibly important for our role as changemakers. Joy helps us immediately bring more spaciousness into our body, mind, and heart and consequently bring back a certain lightness to our efforts. It reminds us of the beauty of life and is an important ingredient to help us turn toward suffering with a sense of equanimity. Cultivating joy can create a new level of happiness in your life and can enable businesses to focus more on satisfying needs rather than fabricating wants.

Joy does not need a big, outer event to happen. Joy creeps in quietly through the cracks in our everyday life experiences. When I asked people what brings them joy, these are some of the things they said: my morning coffee, my pillow, a hug from my partner, being outside in nature, playing the piano, spending time with good friends, seeing my child smile, cooking a meal, buying flowers, cuddling my pet and looking at the sea. It seems that what gives us joy are often the little things that we tend not to make enough time for. Joy evokes a deep sense of satisfaction with life. Cultivating joy in a society where we are made to believe we never are enough or have enough, that we need to be better and have more, is both liberating and revolutionary.

If experiencing joy is so simple, why don't we experience it more often? A few reasons come to mind. First, it seems that we are just too busy to notice the small stuff and pay too much attention to the next big event coming our way. In that sense, mindfulness enhances our ability to experience joy, simply by connecting us with the present moment. Second, we easily confuse joy with pleasure, which tends to be short-lived and often leaves us starving for more. Binge-watching the latest series and spending time on social media are obvious examples of short-lived and somewhat addictive pleasures. Third, and perhaps most surprisingly, we don't allow ourselves to be happy.

I have met several people who would not allow themselves to be happy, and when they were, they felt bad about it. "How can I be happy when other people are suffering so much? It feels wrong," one retreat participant told me. This is something I have noticed particularly with changemakers, who sometimes seem to feel bad for feeling good. While the intention is noble, it is a limiting belief that neither serves our effectiveness as leaders nor eliminates the suffering of others. On the contrary, it creates more suffering. Finally, there seem to be cultural elements rooted in the Protestant work ethic, which places a high value on hard work and the belief that our right to experience joy needs to be earned. When I shared this idea, it usually resonated with my friends from Northern Europe, while my friends from Southern Europe, where the culture is more influenced by Catholicism than Protestantism, stared at me with disbelief.

It is helpful to become aware of what gets in the way of experiencing joy so that you can actively make more room for it in your life. However, sometimes we find ourselves in life circumstances where joy seems very far away. Our hearts are full of sorrow and feel closed to the joy that can come from the things in life that normally make us happy. Gratitude holds the key. A study by Martin Seligman, the father of Positive Psychology, asked people who considered themselves severely depressed to write down three good things that happened to them each day for fifteen days. By the end, 94% of the subjects reported lower levels of depression, and 92% said their happiness increased.[91]

A friend of mine was going through a hard time in his life, feeling pessimistic for weeks. He tried giving it some time and thinking positively, but neither worked. "Finally," he said, "I tried gratitude." Initially, that didn't work either. He told me how he envisioned his daughter, whom he loves very much, but felt no gratitude. His partner, whom he has loved so much for many years—no feeling of gratitude.

He envisioned his work, acknowledging it was meaningful, but felt no feeling of gratitude. "It was really frustrating," he said. But then, all of a sudden, gratitude shone through in a mundane, everyday experience. He continued: "It was like the sky covered with dark clouds suddenly cracked, and through the crack the light got in." It was as if his heart which had felt heavy and closed was now opening up, allowing him to feel a little more spacious and joyful.

There is a secret to gratitude that most people don't tell you. There is a difference between *thinking* what you should be grateful for and *feeling* what you are grateful for in that moment. Gratitude and taking in the goodness are simple and powerful practices to shift the baseline of your happiness. But the key is to approach it without judgment and not to force it. If you tell yourself you are grateful for "having enough to eat" when you've never experienced hunger or poverty, then this is most likely too much of a stretch. You will be in your mind instead of your heart, and that doesn't work. We'll go deeper into how to rewire your brain by taking in the goodness in this week's sidebar.

Cultivating joy and gratitude are powerful ways to counterbalance our natural negativity bias and shift our mind from scarcity to abundance. Moreover, it helps us to balance our nervous system, widen our window of tolerance and keep our hearts open amid the mountain of daily bad news we are exposed to. It allows us to fall back in love with our lives and opens our eyes to the things we have naturally gotten used to and don't pay much attention to anymore. In difficult times, tiny moments of seeing the goodness—taking joy in the sunshine peeking through the leaves, in your morning coffee, or in a warm smile from a stranger—can be the crack that lets new hope and joy come in again.

Becoming Porous

The last of the four wholesome qualities is equanimity, which is our capacity to experience a sense of peace and spaciousness as all things arise and pass. As leaders of change, in the midst of many crises, our ability to stay calm and centered can make all the difference. In these uncertain times, fear and panic can spread easily but if you can stay stable on the inside despite all the turbulence on the outside, you become a lighthouse for those around you.

It is relatively easy to experience peacefulness on the meditation cushion or while we are on retreat, but the real work happens off the cushion. Our meditation is merely a training ground for the real world. I remember, when I first started to meditate, I needed to have everything quiet around me, the less noise on the outside, the less noise on the inside, I thought. Even much later in my practice I remember occasionally getting angry when my husband and kids were too noisy. *How dare they disturb my peace!* A perfect example of what equanimity is not. Today, I know that my ability to experience peace is entirely dependent on my ability to rest in awareness, without clinging to or rejecting whatever arises. It does not depend on any outer circumstances, although some days that is easier and some days it is harder.

Equanimity does not happen overnight. But it is something that we can develop as we gain a deeper understanding of the two wings of mindfulness, wisdom and compassion. By becoming more present, working with our thoughts and emotions, and cultivating wholesome states of being, we can widen our window of tolerance and become a little more porous. It is important to note that each of our journeys is unique: each one of us has their share of pain to transform and the timing of our healing is not always ours to choose. If you are going through a hard time right now and you are already at the edge, then don't push yourself further. You cannot just rip open your window of tolerance. Instead, practice as well as you can to receive the challenges that present themselves with a sense of loving-kindness and compassion. Equanimity will come with increasing wisdom and as you become more comfortable with discomfort.

Resting in equanimity does not mean we don't care. Indifference is rooted in numbness and not being present with what is. I've heard people say "equanimity is not for me. Isn't having strong feelings what makes being human so interesting?" But this is based on a false understanding of what equanimity is. Equanimity is not a withdrawal from life, and it does not mean losing our passion for changing the world or for our favorite sports team. It means that our window of tolerance for holding the pain and the beauty of life gets wider and wider. In my experience, with practice our emotions are better able to move through us and we feel more alive. We might think of 'advanced mindfulness' as some kind of lasting inner peace but the Buddhist nun Pema Chödrön reminds us that "*Enlightened* people are not the ones who do not feel fear, anger, doubt, jealousy, aversion and the like. On the contrary, they have learned to become fully intimate with those emotions and to open their heart to whatever state arises."[92]

Equanimity also involves embracing the impermanence of all things. Understanding that both successes and failures are temporary, that our feelings of glory and shame are just that—temporary feelings—can help us become more courageous and avoid becoming too attached to any one outcome. Seeing our current challenges of humanity in the context of a long history of previous challenges also helps to strengthen our equanimity as we work to create positive impact. Finally, being aware that we only get to live each day in our lives once makes it precious and urgent.

As Jack Kornfield said in our teacher training, "To find peace in the world, we have to find peace in ourselves." Being able to connect with a sense of inner peace not only increases our wellbeing but also has the power to influence the wider world. As we cultivate peace within ourselves, we create ripple effects, fostering environments where others can also find peace, stability and clarity. With equanimity we can stay centered and lead from a place of love rather than fear, even when it is difficult. Sensing our interbeing we can see how our action can spread across the wider web of our relationships.

Increasing Resilience

As our crises continue to unfold, we must become more resilient in dealing with the ups and downs of leading organizations, communities and families. Cultivating an open heart through the practices of loving-kindness, compassion, joy and equanimity will help build this resilience. Rather than viewing your heart as a liability in this highly competitive, often cut-throat and emotionally numb environment, consider it your superpower. It is your heart that helps you reconnect within when you feel lost, mend your relationships with others, and understand that you are not separate from nature.

The concept of resilience originally comes from materials science and refers to an object's ability to adapt and become more stable without losing its original shape when exposed to pressure or stress. Not surprisingly, many of us associate resilience with something rigid and unyielding, phrases like "tough as steel" or "what doesn't kill me makes me stronger" and images of a tall, hundred-year-old oak tree come to mind. For us that often means that we try hard to hold it together, we bottle up our feelings because we are afraid that once we lift the lid, everything will fall apart. Have you ever experienced this? And sometimes, when we are so under pressure, not lifting the lid might be the wise choice. Because we know that when we let ourselves feel all the feelings, we might not have sufficient spaciousness for them all. We might be overwhelmed and fall apart. There are situations in our lives where we need to hold it together to continue to function and be able to lead ourselves and others through a crisis. However, the longer we do that, the more we start to feel disconnected from ourselves, our bodies and our hearts. And the more disconnected we are from ourselves, the harder it is to be connected to others and our environment.

In psychology, resilience refers to our capacity for flexible adaptation—both mentally and emotionally—in the face of stressful or challenging situations. The American Psychological Association describes resilience as "the process of adapting well in the face of adversity, trauma, tragedy, threats or significant sources of stress, such as family and relationship problems, serious health problems, or workplace and financial stressors. Resilience is not a trait that people either have or do not have. It involves behaviors, thoughts and actions that anyone can learn and develop."[93]

Drawing on our insights so far, what if, instead of thinking about resilience as something rigid, resilience was indeed something very flexible? What comes to mind is an image such as water instead of steel. Steel, while strong and seemingly indestructible, is also rigid and unyielding. It can withstand significant force, but once its limit is reached, it can crack or break. In contrast, water is fluid and adaptable.

It can flow around obstacles, seep through the tiniest cracks, and reshape itself to fit any container. Water can be gentle, like a stream, or powerful, like a tsunami. It embodies flexibility and adaptability, continually changing form yet remaining fundamentally the same.

Studies with exiled Tibetan monks who endured political violence, imprisonment, torture and forced resettlement have found them to have remarkable levels of resilience. This high level of resilience has been linked to the qualities of "spaciousness and flexibility" and their ability to use adversity and suffering to generate more wisdom and compassion[94]. Most likely, you and I have a long way to go before we could generate compassion for our torturers, but we can use the practices described in this book to build our resilience, to become more flexible and spacious. Research shows that the practices of loving-kindness and compassion can leave long-term imprints on different regions of the brain responsible for emotional regulation and resilience.

Resilience hence refers to both our ability to pick ourselves up again and recover after difficult and traumatic events, and also our capacity to maintain inner balance under stress, grow in difficult situations, and regain balance after intense physical or mental stimulation. We are all born with the ability to face life again and again. As described at the beginning of this book, we carry an inherent propensity to heal and regenerate from both outer physical and inner psychological wounds. The qualities of our heart provide the nourishing ground from which resilience can grow. As Rick Hanson explains in his book *Resilient*, "True resilience fosters wellbeing, an underlying sense of happiness, love and peace."[95]

Finally, living and leading with a sense of purpose is another crucial piece of the puzzle for achieving greater resilience and happiness. Dedicating our time to something that creates meaning for us gives us additional motivation to use adversity for our growth and makes it easier to experience a sense of peace and satisfaction. In the next chapter and our final week, we will reflect on what that means for you.

WEEK 5–GOING DEEPER: REWIRE YOUR BRAIN WITH GOODNESS

Scientists used to think that the structure of our brains, once we become adults, would be fixed. Now we know that our brains are actually malleable and that we can literally rewire our brain thanks to neuroplasticity. Making it a habit to "Take in the Good," as neuropsychologist Rick Hanson writes in *Buddha's Brain*, is a powerful way to adjust your default mode and thereby increase your happiness and resilience.[96]

Why it works

Although our brain comprises only about 2% of the body's weight, it consumes approximately 20% of the body's oxygen and glucose. It is estimated to contain about one trillion cells, including around a hundred billion neurons, which communicate with each other across junctions called synapses. A typical neuron fires 5-50 times per second. Therefore, while you were reading this, quadrillions of signals traveled through your brain.

What determines the way we are 'wired' is our experiences. Neuroscientists describe this process as: *neurons that fire together wire together*. Additionally, the more often certain neurons fire together, the stronger their wiring becomes. For example, if my default reaction to feeling bored is to check my phone, and this behavior satisfies my underlying need for distraction with a dopamine hit, repeating this many times creates something like a neurological super-highway, which then forms a habit. However, inactive synapses get weaker and can eventually disappear.

Because our brain is "Teflon for good news and Velcro for bad news," as Hanson describes it, it takes active effort to internalize our positive experiences to counterbalance the negative ones. The frequency, duration and intensity of our experiences all influence the strength of the wiring.

How it works

1. **Notice**—use mindfulness to notice positive experiences.

2. **Pause**—just for a few seconds, as if you are capturing this moment in a picture frame.

3. **Let it sink in**—feel it in your body, bathe in the goodness.

Ways to do it

– Make Gratitude a Habit

Make gratitude a part of your daily practice. This can be very informal and take just one or two minutes of your day. Some people like to spend an extra minute in bed before they get up to think about how their life is blessed. Others prefer to take a moment of reflection in the evening to close the day and drift into sleep with gratitude. It is also helpful to integrate gratitude into your meditation practice and reflect on what you are grateful for before you start. You can also deliberately pause a few times a day to notice what you are grateful for. Some people like to write things down, while others prefer to sit in silence. Expressing your gratitude to the people you appreciate is a powerful way to recognize the goodness in your life and spread joy. Try different practices to find the one that suits you best and remember, it must come from your heart, not your mind.

– Find the Crack (where the Light enters) and stay there

Notice moments of kindness and joy as they enter your life in the midst of all the busyness. Perhaps it is a moment of feeling the sunshine on your skin, encouraging words from a work colleague, watching people embrace at the airport, a hug from someone you love or seeing an old couple laughing together. Pause when you notice these cracks of light, allow your heart to be touched and let the goodness sink into your body. You might find it helpful to reinforce the intensity of your experience by using an image, such as rain falling down or soaking up the good feeling like a sponge.

– Look for Counter-Evidence

When you catch yourself thinking of an old limiting belief, deliberately choose to look for counter-evidence and let that sink into your memory. For example, if you think *Everyone is so competitive*, look for evidence of cooperation; if you think *Everyone is greenwashing and no one cares*, look for examples of sincere efforts and caring leaders; if you think *I am all alone*, look for evidence of people supporting you. This way we can nourish and be nourished by the things we want to have more of. Similarly, when you notice your inner critic, replace it with the voice of your inner friend and look for evidence supporting your friend. For example, your critic might say "Work that is not paid for is not real work." Your inner friend might say, "That's bullshit and disparaging of the time we spend supporting our children, elderly and sick. Unpaid work can be very valuable."

Week 5–Questions and Exercises

Questions

- What role does kindness play in your life? Consider your family, friends, the people you work with. What role do you want kindness to play?
- Do you find inner (self-) compassion or outward-focused compassion for others easier? What would help you to balance the two?
- What's the difference between pleasure and joy for you?
- What brings you joy?
- Which one of the four *Radiant Abodes*, (Loving-kindness, Compassion, Joy and Equanimity) speaks to you the most, at this point of your life? Is there one in particular that you would like to bring into your life more?
- What image of resilience do you find most helpful: steel, water, or something else? Why?

Exercises

- As you go about your day, bring in the quality of (loving-) kindness. When you interact with others, writing an email or in a meeting, notice how you feel in your body when you communicate from the heart.
- Next time your Evil Wolf shows up, can you sense its pain? What is it afraid of? And what happens if you turn toward it with kindness and compassion?
- Pay attention to your inner critic, what language it is using and how it makes you feel. Try imagining an 'inner friend': how would it respond?
- Before your meditation today, sit a few moments in silence and let whatever you are grateful for in that moment enter your

awareness. Take your time and feel the sensation in your heart region without judgment. Give thanks, if that feels right for you.

- Do at least one thing today that brings you joy. Appreciate and savor it.
- Continue to use small moments of discomfort to widen your window of tolerance.

Week 5–Daily Meditation

Classic Loving-kindness Meditation (Mettā)

This week's meditation is designed to cultivate an open heart toward ourselves and all beings around us.

Details about accessing this meditation can be found on my website.

https://www.susannevonderbecke.com/consciousimpact/meditation5

A transcript of this meditation can be found in the appendix.

Try to do this meditation three to four times this week. This meditation can take some time to get used to. You can continue with this meditation for as long as you like or alternate it with any of the previous meditations.

Week 5–Optional Breathwork

Coherent Breathing

This breathing practice slows down the breath to between 4.5 and 6.5 breaths per minute, which is considered the optimal frequency for nervous system balance, heart rate variability, oxygen uptake and delivery and other bodily functions. (Most people breathe between nine and twenty-four breaths per minute.)

As you slow down your breathing, let your breath be light and gentle without taking in your usual much larger volume of air. Sit up straight to stay alert and relax your shoulders.

1. Inhale through the nose, slowing it down so that your inhalation lasts five seconds. You can count: "In, 2, 3, 4, 5."
2. Exhale through the nose and slow down your exhalation to last five seconds. You can count: "Out, 2, 3, 4, 5."

If this rhythm feels too forced and leaves you out of breath, you can start with four seconds instead. Similarly, if you want to extend the length of your breath to six seconds, that is also fine. Feel free to try out what works for you, just make sure that your inhalation and exhalation have the same length. Let your breath be soft (don't force it) and continuous (without a long pause in between).

Start with 3–5 minutes per session. If you enjoy the practice, you can extend it over time.

Practice before your meditation or any time during the day.

LEADERSHIP SKILLS
FOR CONSCIOUS IMPACT
Chapter 3
Cultivating Presence & Awareness
Chapter 4
Sensing our Interbeing
Chapter 5
Cultivating an Open Mind
Chapter 6
Being Comfortable with Discomfort
Chapter 7
Cultivating an Open Heart
Chapter 8
Leading with Purpose

CHAPTER 8

WEEK 6 | LEADING WITH PURPOSE

"The most important thing is to remember the most important thing."
Suzuki Roshi

Many business leaders seem to be familiar with the concept of purpose in an organizational context, but I have met few who have taken the time to think about what this means for their personal lives. In my conversations with business leaders, they generally acknowledge the power of purpose to bring alignment across organizational departments, inspire and empower employees to act toward a common goal, and to give a sense of meaning and satisfaction with one's work.

The personal passions and convictions of an organization's leaders, as well as the broader cultural and generational context, influences how its purpose is defined. For most of the last half-century, greed was regarded as good, individual success was measured in money and collective progress in GDP. As Milton Friedman[97] famously argued, the purpose of business is business—and that was enough. Nowadays, shareholder capitalism, at least in theory, has largely given way to stakeholder capitalism defining the purpose and responsibility of a company in a larger social context.[98] Today, "purpose-driven" often implies an intention that goes beyond just making money and is often associated with an additional focus on sustainability, environmental impact, social justice, equality and inclusion and wellbeing. Responses to a 2024 survey show nearly all GenZs and Millennials believe having a sense of purpose is important for their job satisfaction and wellbeing. Moreover, many of them are not afraid to reject an assignment or project based on their personal ethics or beliefs.[99]

Implementing a purpose-led strategy to meet the current *Zeitgeist* and demand by future employees and consumers, however, is like learning to meditate to become more successful in a degenerative system. It misses the opportunity for real transformation. The magnitude and complexity of our current environmental and social challenges requires us to move beyond becoming a little more sustainable, a.k.a., a little less bad. Addressing our outer crises requires us to regenerate the planet, heal ourselves, and find a new way of being with each other and with nature. For this to happen, we need brave leaders who forge the way for new ways of working, collaborating, governing, parenting and caretaking before those new ways become mainstream.

When I talk about your role as a leader, I am not referring to your title or position of power. I am talking about your ability to inspire others to be the best they can be and your willingness to take responsibility for the impact your actions have on yourself, those around you, and the planet. Your leadership does not only encompass your function within an organization. Recall our interbeing within an interconnected web of relationships. The way we show up for our family, friends and community matters also demonstrates our leadership. Our professional and personal action—and our inaction—ripples out and contributes to larger systems change. Leadership has come in many different styles and facets: autocratic, democratic, transactional, servant, visionary, strategic, ethic, agile, authentic, conscious, to name a few. Whatever your leadership style or preference may be, and however many people you are looking to inspire, whether you lead for profit or not, ultimately, we all are leaders of our own lives.

As we take on the responsibility of creating positive change, we must start first and foremost with ourselves. Just as we are not different people at work and at home, the separation of work and life and our pursuit of the perfect balance is flawed. It is based on the premise that our life is separate from work and the notion that when our work is done, we can start enjoying life. For some, this is true. But many of us like to work and we derive meaning and a sense of connection from it. It is where we can bring our gifts into the world, develop our talents, progress as individuals, and contribute to the greater whole. The more we can be the same person professionally and personally, the more authentically we can show up for ourselves and others.

Leading with purpose means living in alignment with who you want to be and with what really matters to you. At the end of our lives, we are unlikely to say, *I wish I could have worked more, made more money and controlled more people*. What we really want is for our lives to have mattered. Leading with purpose helps us do that. As Zen Master Suzuki Roshi said, "The most important thing is to remember the most important thing." What is the most important thing for you? What does it mean to you to lead a life of purpose? This final chapter is dedicated to helping you find some initial answers.

Living with Purpose is a Process

Leslie was hanging upside down in her seat. Almost all the other passengers had left the plane as the heat of the flames drew closer. She was trying to undo her seatbelt, but her pregnant belly was bulging over the straps, and she could not open it. It was supposed to be her last business trip before her maternity leave. "Luckily," she says, smiling, "I was traveling with a colleague, and it was already his second plane crash." Unlike the other passengers, her colleague Eddie was still on the plane, desperately looking for his laptop. He didn't want to repeat the experience of losing it, as he had during his first crash. The situation was serious. Leslie and her unborn baby were stuck, hanging upside down in an airplane on fire. As soon as Eddie spotted her, he abandoned his mission, unbuckled her seatbelt and helped to balance her upright. The two of them escaped the burning plane and Leslie was ushered into a hotel suite, but it wasn't until she got home that doctors could confirm her baby was going to be fine.

"What a terrible situation," I said, sensing the agony she must have experienced. This was not a story that I was expecting to hear as we sat down to prepare for an interview about her personal impact journey at our annual conference. When the plane crash happened, she was working for an NGO in Mozambique, where she helped entrepreneurs to build viable businesses in eco-tourism, textiles, horticulture and business process outsourcing. Knowing how active and successful she has been since the crash over a decade and a half ago, I asked, “Didn’t this experience make you more risk-averse?” I imagined how such a traumatic experience would make someone want to slow down, to reassess their priorities of putting themselves out there to make a positive difference in the world, and live a quieter life. “It took a long time until I could speak about this experience, and it still impacts me,” she said. “I am literally still carrying a scar on my shoulder that reminds me every day. But no, it did not make me more risk-averse. On the contrary, it reminds me that life can be short, and that I want to make it count.”

We all want our lives to matter. From a very early age, I’ve been asking myself: Why am I here? What is the purpose of being alive, and what am I supposed to do? This quest for purpose was not always comfortable. The desire to make a positive difference in the world felt like a burden I did not know how to carry. I wondered where I would be able to find my purpose. Was it in our choice of a profession? Surely, a doctor saving lives would experience a sense of purpose, as would a lawyer fighting for justice, a politician implementing policies to increase the prosperity of a nation, or a CEO leading a company that allows others to earn a good living and provide for their families. These people, I thought, would experience a sense of purpose.

But upon closer inspection, the jobs never seemed as glorious as my teenage mind had imagined. Moreover, they seemed to be other people’s purposes, not mine, which continued to be elusive. Then, I thought, perhaps purpose was not to be found in a profession but in our relationships with others. In the end, how does your life matter if you are a kick-ass successful person but have no friends? How we relate to others, I thought, could provide a clue. Some people, it seemed to me, found a sense of purpose in having children and being with their loved ones. But at that time in my life, I did not see how that had anything to do with changing the world. Finally, it seemed that most wise people would say something like: “There is no purpose, the purpose of life is life itself." It sounded indeed very wise but also utterly impractical for someone deciding what to study to acquire the necessary skills to later find a meaningful job and make a difference.

Sometimes, when none of the options seem to be true, it is because all of the options are true. I was looking for purpose as if it was something to be found or a destination to arrive at. However, purpose is not one thing. It is not that one reason or one task we need to accomplish to avoid wasting our life. Instead, leading a life with purpose is a continuous process of becoming and unbecoming. What gives us a sense of meaning and direction changes with time as we go through different stages in our lives. It is a continuous unfolding of what we do (our goals and the actions we take), why we do it (our intention and the meaning we give it), and how we do it (the values that guide us and our state of being).

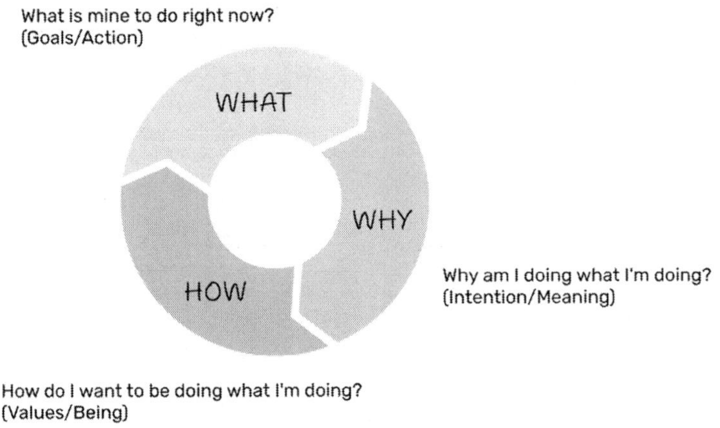

Leading with Purpose is a continuous process of reconnecting with our 'why?', 'how?' and 'what?'

I recently attended an impact conference for business leaders where one of the main speakers, a serial entrepreneur and a legend in the field of sustainability in his seventies, was asked where he sees himself going next. "I don't know," he replied. "It seems every six years I go through an identity crisis where I need to let go of something. I am in the middle of this process right now." Leading with purpose requires us to pause. Sometimes, life provides this pause in the form of a midlife crisis, an illness, or the loss of a loved one, stopping us in our tracks and asking us to remember the most important thing. Alternatively, we can make it our practice to pause once in a while, to see what we need to let go, what wants to emerge, and what matters right now. As we continuously align *what matters* with our actions (the "what"), our intention (the "why"), and our values (the "how"), we will forge a life with purpose.

Creating Meaning through Service

As leading with purpose is a continuous process, there is no beginning and no end. However, let's start with "why" as the inspirational leadership expert Simon Sinek suggests. He writes:

> *"Very few people or companies can clearly articulate WHY they do WHAT they do. By WHY I mean your purpose, cause or belief—WHY does your company exist? WHY do you get out of bed every morning? And WHY should anyone care?"*[100]

As a business leader who wants to change the world, understanding your "why" is crucial. It's about harnessing your strengths, talents and passions to serve others and contribute to their wellbeing. Asking *Why am I doing what I am doing?* can help you reconnect with your intention and with what matters in a given situation. When our intention is based on being of service to the greater whole, our action becomes meaningful to others. Intention is at the heart of mindfulness, which allows us to move from habitual reactions to an intentional response. Being more intentional in your relationships with those around you, and with yourself, can inspire others and help you transform your life.

In an international survey of over two million individuals across 500 different jobs, those who reported the most meaning in their careers were clergy, teachers, school administrators, surgeons, therapists, chiropractors, and psychiatrists. All of these roles focus on promoting physical, mental or spiritual health. Being of service does not mean that you constantly meet other people's needs and wishes. It means that we tend to experience a sense of purpose and satisfaction when our action impacts those around us in a positive way.[101]

Interestingly, many of these roles aren't highly paid. It seems to be symptomatic of our economic system that doing good does not always correlate with doing well (economically speaking). Additionally, there is other work that is often described as highly demanding, nerve-racking, and not paid at all: parenting our children and taking care of sick family members. Yet, it is something that is often described as being meaningful. Taking care of each other honors our interbeing and need for belonging.

The other benefit of creating meaning through service is that it helps you to overcome obstacles on your journey and persevere in the long run. Being a changemaker can be a lonely experience. It can be highly frustrating when we seem to be running out of time and when economic and political short-term interests get in the way of long-term investments. However, when your intention is not only to benefit yourself but also others, your motivation can become bigger than your fears or anger and it propels you forward in difficult times.

Psychologist, researcher and professor Angela Duckworth shares the following story in her book *Grit: Why Passion and Resilience are the Secrets to Success*:

> *"Three bricklayers are asked: 'What are you doing?' The first says, 'I am laying bricks.' The second says, 'I am building a church.' And the third says, 'I am building the house of God.' The first bricklayer has a job. The second has a career. The third has a calling."*

She finds that only a minority of people consider their work a calling but that "those who do are significantly grittier." She continues to explain that those fortunate people who see their work as a calling "reliably say 'my work makes the world a better place.' And it's these people who seem most satisfied with their jobs and their lives overall."[102]

This sense of service and interconnection is also found in the Buddhist tradition of becoming a Bodhisattva, which means making a vow to wake up not just for oneself but for the welfare of all beings.

The causes we are drawn to and feel passionate about are often inspired by our personal experiences, stories and suffering. However, sometimes we cannot explain why we are drawn to one cause more than another. Whether it is human rights, animal rights, reforestation, conservation, climate, biodiversity, farming, education or whatever you feel drawn to, the way that you can contribute will depend on your skills, resources and unique personal situation at a given time.

When considering which problems to dedicate our time and resources to, it is easy to get lost in the complexity of the tasks at hand and feel overwhelmed by the world's needs. In that case, it may be helpful to start with yourself and ask: What makes me come alive? Howard Thurman, an American Civil Rights Leader, advised: "Don't ask yourself what the world needs; ask yourself what makes you come alive, then go do that. Because what the world needs is people who have come alive." I believe this to be true. We have to start with ourselves and trust that by unfolding our full potential, in service to wellbeing, we become the pieces of the puzzle of the change we want to see.

Values as Your Guide into the Unknown

The second element of leading with purpose is knowing your values, asking yourself, *How do I want to be doing what I am doing?* As we face a multitude of crises and our external circumstances are constantly changing, planning and achieving goals becomes more difficult. When everything is uncertain, values can guide us in deciding which options to pursue and which steps to take. They help us act in alignment with our hearts and who we want to be as we lead ourselves and others into the unknown future.

While knowing our intention creates meaning by reestablishing our connection to the world through a sense of service, embodying the values that matter to us makes the simple act of 'being' meaningful. When we are aligned with our values, reaching our goals becomes secondary because the journey itself is already meaningful. At the end of each day and at the end of our lives, we are less likely to have regrets and more likely to have lived a life that we can be proud of, regardless of what we may or may not have achieved in the world.

Knowing how we want to *be* is different from what you typically read about in business school literature. This 'how' is not about how you get from A to B, focusing on the external structures and processes you need to reach your goals. Instead, it concerns your state of being while you figure out how to get from A to B—your internal compass that helps you create change from a place of love, rather than fear. Acting within an invisible web of relationships, the quality of how we interact matters.

The author James Clear, who wrote the bestseller *Atomic Habits: An Easy & Proven Way to Build Good Habits & Break Bad Ones*, lets values guide him in order to make better long-term choices while addressing short-term problems:

> *"One of the solutions I've been trying out is to let my values drive my choices. That doesn't mean I ignore other aspects of my decision-making process. I simply add my core values into the mix. For example, if I'm working on a problem in my business, rather than just asking, 'Will this make money?' I can ask, 'Is this in alignment with my values?' And then, 'Will this make money?' If I say no to either, then I look for another option."*[103]

The four Brahmaviharas—loving-kindness, compassion, joy and equanimity—are expressions of such personal values. There might be others that inspire you. I have yet to meet someone who says their values are deception, imbalance, injustice, ignorance, confusion, cowardice, hatred, conflict, cruelty, or indifference. Personal values are more likely to be authenticity, peace, optimism, fairness, clarity, courage, generosity, care, respect, responsibility, honesty and so on. The qualities that inspire and nourish us are essentially derivatives of love and wisdom.

Perhaps you noticed that while reading these words, your body reacted and felt a certain way. Reading the first set of words likely felt contractive, while reading the second set of words felt more expansive. The values that matter to you will influence your state of being and, hence, how you feel while you are in action. As discussed in the previous chapter, cultivating wholesome states of mind can shift your brain's default mode and baseline happiness. Moreover, they increase your resilience and capacity to be with both the pain and the beauty, which is crucial for our effectiveness as changemakers. When you are living your values, anchored in the expression of your loving heart, you become an inspiration for yourself and others.

I found it helpful to write down those values that reflect how I want to be in my professional life, as a spouse and as a parent. This exercise was illuminating because, before doing that, I did not realize that certain values were more important to me than others. Being aware of them helps me cultivate what brings me a sense of satisfaction and joy, and it has been helpful in guiding me back to what matters when I feel stressed or lost. Knowing how you want to be and feel helps you create a vision for your life that matters to you and can help us create a new way of being in the world.

Without taking the time to pause and reflect, most of us don't really know what values matter to us most. Everything might sound important. But when you *do* take a closer look, you may find that some values resonate more with you and that they are exactly what you need in order to develop your full potential and express who you are. It is possible that some values will accompany you throughout your life, while others may change with different life stages and circumstances.

Becoming Love in Action

The final element of leading your life with purpose is to identify your goals and take action, asking yourself, *What is mine to do right now?* Rooted in our intention to serve and guided by our values, we are essentially opening ourselves to becoming love in action.

When you are in the middle of a planetary emergency, weather changes, pandemics, social conflict, mass migration, and new technologies make planning a lot more difficult. You can make a five-year-plan for your business or personal life but when it comes to breaking down big dreams into all the individual steps that will take you there, you will find that it requires a lot of adjustments, flexibility and teamwork. When you look at important goals you've set for yourself, is it possible that even if you've been able to realize them, the path to get there turned out to be quite different from what you had imagined it to be?

Life has always been uncertain, but the complexity of today's challenges and the fast pace of change today means that leading ourselves and others into the future can be like driving in the dark. When we cannot see ahead very far, when we are navigating in unknown territory, planning becomes more difficult and sensing our next step becomes increasingly important. Asking yourself *What is mine to do, right now?* is about sensing the right course of action.

Sensing requires you to reconnect with your body, quiet the mind, and reconnect with your heart. It taps into the inherent intelligence of life, into our collective field of awareness and then expresses itself through your unique character, abilities and talents. Sensing what is ours to do in a given situation helps us to do what we can and not get overwhelmed by the magnitude of the problems we are trying to solve. It can give us back a sense of agency by taking away the pressure caused by thinking that we have to, or even can, fix the enormous problems alone while acknowledging that we have a part to play that is uniquely ours.

The big situations in life that determine whether or not we have lived our lives with purpose are not confined to our work. If we want to make this world a better place, then we should be equally intentional about our actions in our personal lives. I believe that those of us who have the ability to create positive change, because of our good fortune and relative position of influence, also have the responsibility to dedicate ourselves to some of the larger issues we face as humans on this planet. However, let's not forget the ones closest to us. Our ability to effect positive change is not limited to where we work. It is possible to connect to a sense of purpose also through volunteering for non-profit organizations, supporting projects within your community, or spending very deliberate time with your family. Sometimes we can get so occupied with our role as a leader and changemaker in the world that we forget to ask *What is mine to do at home, with my family and my local community?* Isn't it there that it all starts?

One of the difficulties you may encounter in defining your goals and actions is that you want to do too much. Looking at the areas of impact in our lives, we want to spend meaningful time with our family, make a difference at work, be part of a community, and create positive change for the environment and society. If this is you, I get it. We want to do everything right and be the best person we can. The danger is that we start to spread ourselves too thin, stop being effective and run out of energy. There is a second part to the question of sensing *What is mine to do?* and that is *What is mine to do, right now?* Sometimes, life asks us to focus on one area of our life in particular.

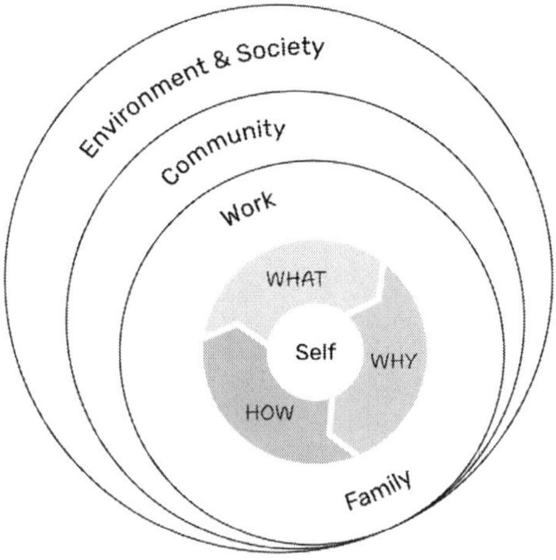

Leading with purpose creates ripples through our interbeing with others

The currency of your life is not money, it is time. Allocating your time to action that is meaningful and creates a positive impact for yourself and others is essential when you lead your life with purpose. This process is probably as much about sensing what to do as it is about knowing what not to do. Saying *no* to what doesn't matter is at least as important as saying *yes* to what is. Your meditation is a training ground for moving from autopilot to conscious response so that you can choose action that is in alignment with what matters to you.

Taking stock and re-adjusting your time to spend it on activities aligned with your sense of purpose can be both exciting and scary. If your work feels more like doing a job than following your calling, does it mean you have to quit? I don't know. What do you think? For some jobs, the world would be better off without them. But not everybody has the luxury to choose. Financial and personal dependencies can take that option from us. Moreover, research shows that our passion for something often grows as we learn and become more proficient in what we do.[104] In some cases, sticking with our job, and making it meaningful as we master it, can be the way.

Sensing what is ours to do right now requires us to use a part of our brain that we seem to have forgotten how to use. While the left part of our brain is great in finding solutions to problems in a system that resembles a machine—imagine a watch or an assembly line—which require linear thinking focused on the individual parts, the right side of our brain is better at finding solutions to complex problems, which require non-linear systemic thinking and a focus on the greater whole.

Interestingly, what activates the right side of your brain is in many ways what reconnects you to a sense of joy, playfulness, creativity and awe. Zen Master Suzuki Roshi not only urged us to "Remember the most important thing," he also told us "What we are doing here is so important, we better not take it too seriously." Your mindfulness practice can help you find a new balance in your thinking and being that will allow you to lead your life with purpose and create change from a place of love and connection.

Letting Go: Too Important to Be Serious

Ironically, in order to make the world a better place, we need to stop wanting to make her a better place. We need to accept and fall in love with her just the way she is. In order to live your life with purpose, you have to find purpose and let it go again. When we cling to our purpose, we lose the inner spaciousness that allows us to be in co-creation with life as it unfolds. Letting go is essential to living with purpose because it allows us to become a vehicle for change where what matters is the impact it creates and not *who* creates that impact. We need to set goals in order to take action toward longer-term objectives—and be ready to abandon them and create new ones as the circumstances change. We need to be guided by our values, knowing that they are not the only truths. Finally, we need to be rooted in our intention to be of service, knowing that a good intention does not guarantee a good outcome.

In our inner work, it is the same. In order to widen our capacity to be with pain and beauty, with the unpleasant and the pleasant, we must accept the present moment exactly as it is, so that we are then able to let it go. As we give up our hope for a better past and allow ourselves to feel and heal, we are able to create a different future. The work is never done. It is a continuous becoming and unbecoming, moving in layers, moving in circles, never linear. We need a sense of self, our ego, to become *somebody* so we can then let go and become *nobody*. I mean becoming nobody in the sense that we no longer cling to, and over-identify with, the different roles we play in our lives, including the role of being (or wanting to be) a changemaker or a leader. In our meditation we can experience the nature of our awareness—that part of us which is always there whilst everything else is changing—as emptiness. Emptiness, as you may recall, is not nothing: emptiness is full of potential. Therefore, in order to live our full potential as changemakers we must do our best and let go and become empty.

Organizational psychologist and professor at Wharton University, Adam Grant describes in his book *Think Again: The Power of Knowing What You Don't Know,*[105] how his students usually go through the following evolution of self-esteem in their careers: "Phase 1: I'm not important. Phase 2: I'm important. Phase 3: I want to contribute something important." As we become experts in our fields, it is easy to get stuck in Phase 2. We see everything through the lens of what we know. In my case, that meant going through quite a long phase where I thought everybody needs to meditate and everybody needs to make this world a better place. For quite a while, I had no patience for anybody who thought differently. Phase 3, in my experience, is a natural evolution of the idea that the more we learn, the more we realize how much we don't know.[106] Adam Grant adds that he noticed that the sooner his students get to Phase 3, "the more impact they have and the more happiness they experience." When our impact journey is less about ourselves, we experience more joy and become better instruments of change. The more we can let go, the more effective we are in creating change from a place of interbeing and with humility rather than isolated individualism and over-importance.

Week 6–Going Deeper: Meeting a Wise Being—Your Future Self

The following guided reflection is designed to connect you with the wisdom of your heart, helping you to uncover what matters to you right now. We are going to meet a wise being. For me, she is *she*, but the wise being you meet could be *he*, or *they*. Please find a sitting position that allows you to be alert, with a straight spine and also relaxed. Take a few full breaths… then let your breath come naturally. Keep your attention on your breath to allow your mind to settle in this present moment.

Imagine you are walking along a beautiful path. Nature is all around you, the sun is shining. As you walk happily along you approach a house; it is the house of a wise being. Imagine her however you like; she could also even be your future self, about twenty years from now.

You walk up the little path to the house and knock on the door. After a short moment, the wise being opens the door, she smiles at you and invites you into her space.

You notice the living room, the shapes, the colors. And you pass the kitchen—is it clean or messy? You are in the mood to notice these details—and then she invites you to sit down with her on her terrace.

She looks at you and smiles. What do you notice about the way she speaks and about how she's listening to you? How does her presence feel? What values come to your mind?

You talk about life, and you have a question for her. You ask: How do I get to where you are now?

Notice that her answer may come as words, feelings, images or gestures. The answer could be symbolic or literal.

Finally, you may ask her one last question. Thinking of a currently challenging situation in your life, you ask her: What else do you want me to know?

Ask your question and listen with an open heart and mind. Trust that you will understand. If not now, then later.

As your time together is up, the wise being lovingly brings you back to the door. She wishes you farewell and gives you a little gift to remember her. What is it?

Don't overthink this. Go with whatever comes first to your mind, if nothing comes to your mind just focus on the sensation of gratitude for having received this gift of wisdom. You are feeling grateful for the gift of wisdom.

Finally, you say your final goodbyes. You close the door behind you and walk back the way you came, surrounded by nature; the sun is warming your skin, the wind is blowing gently and lifting your spirit. You feel loved and free.

You walk all the way back, until you arrive in the city and the place you are sitting in. Notice your body touching the surface, sense your breath. Slowly you become aware of your surroundings, the birds outside, any sounds around you. You can still feel the presence of this wise being in your heart.

Take a moment to acknowledge what is present for you right now. Perhaps images came to you easily. Note the qualities of being in the presence of the wise being and the corresponding values that inspire you. You may also want to write down the answers to your questions. Maybe you found this exercise difficult, then this is fine too. It is just one possible way to access your inner knowing.

Week 6–Questions and Exercises

Questions

Clarifying your WHY (intention and meaning)

- What makes you come alive – what issues, topics, practices fascinate you?
- What do you consider your five best talents? (Talents are like a gift, something you find easy.) What do these talents help others to do?
- What are your best strengths – characteristics that can be developed, e.g. tenacity, patience, curiosity?
- How do these strengths help you overcome adversity?
- Which talents and strengths give you the most joy or satisfaction?
- What does success mean to you, at this point in your life?

Clarifying your HOW (values and being)

- How do you want to be remembered when you are dead? What do you want people to say about you?
- You are ninety years old and look back at your life as you are leading it right now. How would you finish the following sentences:
- I spent too much time worrying about…
- I spent too little time doing things like…
- If I could do it differently, I would…
- As you think of people in your life or leaders that you admire, what are the qualities that you like most in them?

- What values are most important to you in your different areas of impact: self, work, family, community, environment and society?

Clarifying your WHAT (goals and action)

- How would you complete this sentence:

If I had only 10 more years to live, I would…

- In your role as a changemaker, what do you feel called to do right now?
- Considering your areas of impact—self, work, family, community, environment and society—is there an area that you currently want to focus more, or less, on?
- What are three goals that you want to achieve in alignment with your values and intention to serve? Think of different time frames, for example, the next five years, three years, one year.
- What three things can you do this week to get a little closer to your goals and vision?

Exercises

- Pick the questions that you find most helpful from above and write down your answers, reflecting on your WHY, HOW, and WHAT. Schedule time this week to reflect on what leading with purpose means to you at this stage in your life.
- Reach out to someone close to you and talk to them about their vision (hopes, dreams, aspirations) for the future—for themselves, for others and for the planet.
- Initiate a conversation about what a business, economy, political system that is in service to wellbeing could look like? Listen more than you talk. Practice staying present, with an open mind and heart.

- As you encounter a challenging situation at work or in your personal life, reconnect with your intention and your values to guide your response. Notice the inner and outer impact that creates.
- Complete this sentence:

I want to… (your contribution based on what you love doing), so that… (the impact you want it to have on others).

You can apply this to your different areas of impact.

Week 6–Daily Meditation

Meditation on Resting in Open Awareness

This week's meditation is designed to experience an openness in which all sensations can arise and pass.

Details about accessing this meditation can be found on my website.

https://www.susannevonderbecke.com/consciousimpact/meditation6

A transcript of this meditation can be found in the appendix.

You can practice this the whole week or alternate it with any of the previous meditations.

Week 6–Optional Breathwork

Euphoric Breathing with Breath Hold

This last breathing practice is helpful to access your subconscious and connect with your intuition and creativity. In contrast to the previous exercises, this practice is activating. It can get you into a euphoric state, similar to what can be experienced in deep meditative absorption or longer breath-journeys. If you are prone to dizziness, it may be best to start this practice lying down. Once you are more experienced, you can also try this in a seated position.

Begin by taking a deep breath to relax and connect with your body. When you are ready, begin the sequence: fifteen rounds of connected breathing, followed by a breath-hold and exhalation.

1. Inhale deeply through your mouth: first into your belly, then expand into your chest. Exhale effortlessly through the mouth. At the end of your exhalation, there is no pause, immediately start with the next inhalation.

   Repeat this 15 times.

   After the last exhalation:

2. Inhale deeply and hold your breath (30 seconds or as needed).
3. Exhale slowly through the mouth with slightly pursed lips.

Go through five cycles.

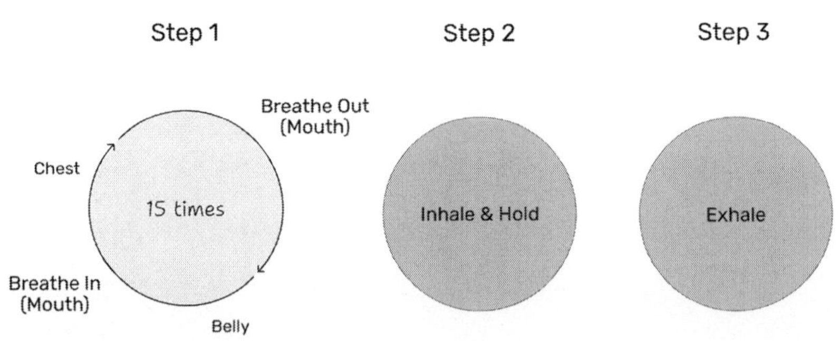

After the last cycle, breathe naturally. Take your time to sit in stillness, feel and enjoy.

Practice in the morning or during the day when you feel tired and in need of a reset. This practice is activating—do not practice when you want to calm down and relax.

CONCLUSION

Congratulations, you made it this far! By now, your body will probably have started to remember what meditating feels like, and it should be getting easier for you. I hope you've gained some valuable insights. My intention was to provide you, along with some theoretical inputs, with a toolbox of practices in the form of meditations, breathwork, and exercises that will help you on your journey of creating positive change in the world. In this final chapter, let's talk about where to take it from here.

First, let's focus on your mindfulness practice. When you get off track, don't dwell on it—simply start again. Carve out a little extra time most days of the week for your inner work. For me, meditation is the foundation that gives me the most benefit in terms of focus, insight, and reconnection with what matters. Breathwork is optional for me, but it may be different for you. My suggestion is to pick a couple of your favorite practices and stick with those. The meditations are thematic. You can use general practices like meditating on the breath, on the body, or in open awareness, and specific themes like interbeing, thoughts and emotions, or Mettā when you want to work on those areas specifically.

Second, regarding your impact journey, I have intentionally refrained from giving specific advice on what to do. What you can do is very specific to your current professional and personal situation. You've likely heard about various options to live more sustainably: lowering your carbon footprint, consuming less and more responsibly, volunteering for local or global organizations and becoming politically active. Depending on your line of work, there may be various ways you could make your business more regenerative over time and you will know this better than me. We can team up with others, found new ventures, or support existing ones. Our journeys of creating positive change in the world can take so many different shapes. There are also many ways to educate ourselves and seek out expertise in specific fields of interest. In fact, you might already know much more than me. Whatever steps you and I have already taken, we can probably do more. Most of us can do more. We must be ambitious and at the same time patient. Our inner and outer work is a journey—a journey of learning, unlearning, healing, being, doing and becoming.

Third, this journey is best taken together. Only you can do your inner work, but you don't have to do it alone. Whether it is your mindfulness practice or your journey of creating positive change in the world, we have so much to learn from each other. Remember, our human superpower as a species has been large-scale cooperation. I am convinced that together we can do this. Let yourself be inspired and don't hold back on inspiring others. You can join online programs, organizations, and physical gatherings—there are many ways to find your tribe and also ways to engage with those who think differently. Going on retreats is a great way to deepen your meditation practice or dedicate time to your inner healing work. Together, we will find a new way of being and working that will be in harmony with each other and the planet.

Fourth, stay in your lane. One thing I noticed when I started practicing, as well as with my co-teachers and students, is that as we become more mindful, we often notice how everyone else around us is not mindful and should be more mindful. Whenever you notice yourself getting upset about how non-mindful or non-sustainable someone else is, make this situation your practice, laugh at yourself, and get back in your lane. You can make everything a practice to strengthen your two wings of mindfulness: compassion and wisdom.

Finally, trust the process. Whether your word is optimism, hope, possibilism, or something else, the opportunity we have as humans at this moment is huge—it's about redefining what we want humanity to be about. We cannot know what will happen in the future, whether we will make it or how, but we can do our best to remember the most important thing. Be courageous in facing the pain in the world and in ourselves, and cultivate joy and kindness to honor the beauty in this world. Let's make this journey one of love and connection, and let ourselves be surprised by the beautiful world that can emerge. I am no longer scared to be called naïve or a dreamer. We don't need the whole world to change. Research in systems thinking has shown that when a system is far from equilibrium, small islands of coherence can be enough to shift the entire system into a new state.[107] Or, if you ever doubt that you can make a difference, these words that I first heard from Jack Kornfield during our teacher training may help you remember: "If you think you're too small to change anything, you've never been in bed with a mosquito."

Thank you for being on this journey together.

APPENDIX

WEEK 1 MEDITATION: TRANSCRIPT OF THE MEDITATION ON THE BODY

Please find a sitting position that is comfortable and where you can also keep your spine straight. If you can, I recommend that you sit on a chair or on a cushion with your hips higher than your knees. Balancing your spine freely without support will help you stay alert. However, if this position creates too much tension in your body, you can try to lie down or lean your back against a wall or chair. I also recommend turning off your devices and, if needed, let other people know not to disturb you during the next twenty minutes.

START

In this meditation you are training to become more present and aware of the sensations in your body. This embodied presence is the basis for leading change from a place of connection and deliberate response. For just a few minutes allow yourself the radical act of slowing down and feeling the present moment.

Now, close your eyes and take one or two long, deep breaths, in through the nose and out through the mouth. Then let your breath come naturally. Relax into the breath.

PAUSE

Bring your attention to where you most easily detect the breath, or perhaps where it's most pleasurable… It could be around your nostrils, or it could be your chest as it moves gently with each inhalation and each exhalation. For this practice, let this place be the anchor of your focus, the home base you return to when you notice your thoughts drifting.

PAUSE

Notice this breath… right here.

PAUSE

If this feels right for you, you can also place your hands on your chest or belly, or both and focus on the sensation of your hands moving with each inhalation and exhalation. Any time your arms get heavy, place them gently and slowly on your lap.

Now, with a relaxed, interested attention, discover what the sensations of the breath feel like, moment to moment. Let the breath come naturally, easily…

As you are breathing in and breathing out…

PAUSE

Where is your attention now? Our minds love wandering off into the future or into the past. This is normal. When you notice your attention drifting off… pause… and gently guide your attention back to the inflow and outflow of your breath. Holding your experience with curious, playful, and perhaps kind, attention.

PAUSE

Now, keep your focus on the breath but expand your attention to include other sensations in your body. Imagine scanning your body from top to toe. Whenever possible, try to soften and release areas of physical tension.

Relax your face. Imagine you could soften the skin around your head, releasing any tension around your jaw. Let your tongue and your lips rest softly.

Now move with your attention to your shoulders… are they heavy, tight, light? Can you relax them a little more?

Notice how your arms and hands feel… is there warmth or coolness, a tingling or a numbness? If you cannot feel much, that is fine, too.

Now come with your attention to your belly… is it soft or tight? Can you let go of tension a little more?

Feel the weight of your body resting on your seat or floor, your feet and legs connecting to the floor, to this earth.

PAUSE

Notice any sensations that are predominant… and then ask: Can I be with this? With a soft, open awareness, feel the sensation as it is…

notice… is it pleasant or unpleasant? How does it change over time? Does it get more intense? Less intense? Perhaps it is changing into another sensation.

If you encounter difficult sensations, strong sensations that you find hard to be with, try to breathe into the sensation. Sometimes the breath can create a certain openness and space.

It can also be helpful to name the sensations, seeing if there is a word that describes your experience: tightness, ache, heat, tingling… Sometimes naming what is present allows us to be with whatever is present in that moment.

PAUSE

Whenever you feel your mind wandering off, or find it difficult to stay present, you can always return to your anchor, focusing on your breath.

Sensing your breath, with a calm, steady attention…

If you feel a strong sensation arising and calling for your attention, let the concentration on your breath recede into the background and expand your attention to whatever is arising… naming what you notice, offering your presence. If nothing strong is calling your attention, continue to rest with your home base… relaxed and alert.

PAUSE

Breathing in and breathing out…

PAUSE

We are learning to be centered, balanced, and present with the waves of sensations that are coming and going in this constantly changing, sometimes intense and difficult but also incredibly beautiful life.

Let us rest here for another minute or so.

PAUSE

Now, slowly become aware of your surroundings again, feeling the presence of your body in the place that you are in, becoming aware of any sounds around you, noticing the presence of other people, life and nature around you… And when you are ready, you may slowly and gently open your eyes again.

END

Week 2 Meditation:
Transcript of the Meditation on Interbeing

Please find a sitting position that is comfortable and where you can also keep your spine straight. If you can, I recommend that you sit on a chair or on a cushion with your hips higher than your knees. Balancing your spine freely without support will help you stay alert. However, if this position creates too much tension in your body, you can try to lie down or lean your back against a wall or chair. I also recommend turning off your devices and, if needed, let other people know not to disturb you during the next twenty minutes.

START

Welcome to this twelve-minute journey of training your awareness to sense your profound interconnectedness with all of life. Remembering our interdependence forms the foundation for creating change from a place of interbeing, rather than separation.

Begin by gently closing your eyes. Take a few deep breaths, in through your nose and out through your mouth. Then let your breath come naturally. Relax into the breath.

PAUSE

Stay with your attention on the breath.

PAUSE

Feel each inhalation and exhalation as they unfold. Perhaps you can notice the coolness of the air as you breathe in and the warmth as you breathe out. Feel the gentle rise of your abdomen and chest with each inhalation and the corresponding release with each exhalation.

PAUSE

Feel your whole body breathing. Notice any area of tension in your body and see if you can relax a little more. Each inhalation automatically creates a little more spaciousness and each exhalation and helps you to release what you no longer need.

PAUSE

Staying anchored in your breath, I'd like to invite you to contemplate our interbeing with nature.

Perhaps you are surrounded by nature right now. Notice if you can hear the sound of nature, the chirping of a bird, the humming of an insect, or leaves rusting in the wind. You can also use your memory to connect with the sense of being in nature.

Feel the sensations of your clothes touching your skin, keeping you warm and comfortable. They too are made from nature, with materials provided by plants and animals.

Did you have anything to drink or eat this morning? Perhaps you drank some water, provided by nature, keeping you hydrated, keeping you alive. Maybe you had a delicious coffee, tea, or juice? All of them grew from the earth with just the right mix of sunlight, rain, and air, and are now giving us nourishment, energy, and joy.

Nature is around you all the time, even inside you. Your food grows on this earth. Your clothes are made from fibers harvested from living plants and animals. The building that you live in and which shields you from the sun, rain and wind is constructed with materials shaped by these elements. Even this meditation, whether you are reading it digitally or on paper, or listening to it on a phone, is powered by nature.

PAUSE

Now ask yourself: Who would I be without nature?
Who would I be without nature?

PAUSE

Without nature, we would not be. We are part of nature and nature is part of us.

PAUSE

If you wish to give thanks to the Earth, you can do so now. Don't worry about finding the right words, just do what comes naturally.

PAUSE

Reconnect with your breath. Notice how you feel. We are not looking for any special experience, only to make room to be with whatever is present for you right now.

Feeling each inhalation and exhalation as they come and go.

PAUSE

Now, let's take a moment to reflect on our interbeing with others.

Notice the surface you are sitting on, a chair, a cushion, or perhaps the floor. If you have your eyes closed you can open them gently, and with a soft gaze notice the material it is made of, its shape and color. Who made this for you? And whose idea was it to make such a thing?

Close your eyes again and visualize the food and drink you were appreciating earlier. There are people who have produced your tea, coffee, or juice. Most likely, you don't know them, but you know of them. Perhaps you can see them in your mind, planting seeds, harvesting, processing. All of them have parents, like you. Some of them have children. Like you, they want to live a happy life. And although they may be far away, in a small way they have touched your life, and you touched theirs.

Now consider your own parents. It doesn't matter right now if you had a good or a difficult relationship with them. They gave you life, opportunities and lessons that shaped who you are today. Our ancestors, grandparents, great-grandparents, and so on, each shaped the next generation, with their hopes and dreams, with their fears and share of suffering.

Finally, I invite you to think of the many benefactors you have had in your life. Some may have come from your inner circle, your friends and family, but others might have been strangers, teachers, doctors, or work colleagues that touched your life in a significant way. Maybe you have had a furry friend that has influenced your life in a positive way.

PAUSE

Now again, I invite you to ask yourself: Who would I be without others?

Who would I be without others?

PAUSE

Without others, we would not be. I am part of you and you are part of me.

PAUSE

If you feel the wish to give thanks to the benefactors in your life, known and unknown, then you can do so now. Again, don't worry about finding the right words, just do what comes naturally.

PAUSE

And so, we are all interconnected in widening circles of relationships, across space and time.
Shaping each other's lives and the world around us.

PAUSE

Let's stay in silence for the last few minutes.

PAUSE

Whenever you notice your mind wandering, which it will, gently guide your attention back to your breath. Feeling your whole body breathing.

Sensing the whole world breathing.

PAUSE

Now, slowly become aware of your surroundings again. Feel your body touching the surface you are sitting on. Become aware of any sounds around you, noticing the presence of other people, life, and nature around you… And when you are ready, gently open your eyes again.

END

Week 3 Meditation: Transcript of the Meditation on Thoughts and Emotions

Please find a sitting position that is comfortable and where you can also keep your spine straight. If you can, I recommend that you sit on a chair or on a cushion with your hips higher than your knees. Balancing your spine freely without support will help you stay alert. However, if this position creates too much tension in your body, you can try to lie down or lean your back against a wall or chair. I also recommend turning off your devices and if needed, let other people know not to disturb you during the next twenty minutes.

START

Welcome to this meditation exploring your thoughts and emotions. Our intention during this meditation is to observe with an interested and kind attention and to be present with whatever thoughts and emotions arise. If you find yourself overwhelmed by very difficult emotions or memories, you can always bring your attention back to your breath, open your eyes and focus on something that nourishes you (for example, nature, a picture, sound…).

Let's begin. Close your eyes and take a couple of deep breaths. Then let your breath come naturally.

Bring your attention to where you most easily detect the breath: your nose, chest or belly, or perhaps where it's most pleasurable… let this place be the anchor for your practice, the place to return to when you notice yourself getting caught up in the content of your thoughts.

Notice your breath, follow the beginning of your inhalation all the way until the end of your exhalation. Each inhalation creates more spaciousness and each exhalation helps you relax a little more.

PAUSE

Now start to mentally scan your body, letting go of any tension in your face, your jaw, relaxing your shoulders, softening your belly. Noticing your legs and feet touching the floor.

Noticing the sensation of your body breathing, moment to moment. Let the breath be easy, no need to direct it in any way.

PAUSE

Now, keep your focus on the breath and expand your attention to notice your thoughts.

In order to stay present, it can be helpful to name each thought as it arises. You may find yourself planning, rehearsing, commenting or judging.

PAUSE

Notice that your thoughts naturally come and go. Your thoughts may come as words or as images, with audio or without, in color or in black and white. What does your thought landscape look like?

PAUSE

You practice observing your thoughts with a curious and kind attention. Letting all thoughts come and go. Noticing and naming as they arise, then letting them go.

PAUSE

We get easily caught up in the storyline of our thinking… when you notice this has happened, you can return to presence by noticing your breath.

Then once more, start observing your thoughts again…coming and going in different shapes and sizes, like clouds in the sky.

PAUSE

Perhaps you notice that your thoughts are often accompanied by emotions. How does planning, rehearsing, commenting, or judging feel? Where do you feel this emotion in your body?

PAUSE

When a thought arises accompanied by a strong emotion, it may be helpful to name this too… You may encounter emotions like worry, restlessness, doubt, or boredom. Perhaps you encounter emotions like excitement, joy, happiness, a sense of peacefulness. Everything is welcome.

PAUSE

Notice what emotions are present for you in this moment, allow them to be as they are, without judgment, holding your experience with curiosity and kindness.

Let us stay here a little longer… observing your thoughts passing by like clouds in the sky, noticing any associated emotions in your body.

PAUSE

When a strong emotion arises, you can ask yourself: Can I be with this? With a soft, open awareness, feel the sensation as it is… notice… how does it change over time? Does it get more intense? Less intense? Is it pleasant, unpleasant, or neutral?

It is possible that you may have difficulty feeling your emotions. Sometimes, it takes time to reconnect with inner feelings and to find the right words. Instead of naming, you can ask yourself: what does this emotion look like? Is there any color or shape to it?

PAUSE

When your mind starts drifting and you become entangled in the content of your thinking, simply return with your focus to your breath.

Our mind is built to think. Thinking can be wonderful, creative, and often useful. Our aim here is not to get rid of our thinking but to avoid getting caught in it. Observing our thoughts, we can see that not all of them are helpful or true.

Witnessing the changing nature of your thoughts and emotions, you become less identified with them. Letting them pass by creates more spaciousness, openness, and freedom.

PAUSE

Now, in these last few minutes of this meditation, bring your attention back to your breath. Let your thoughts and emotions recede into the background, sense the movement of your breath. Noticing the simple freedom of breathing and witnessing.

PAUSE

Now, slowly become aware of your surroundings again. Feel your body touching the surface you are sitting on. Become aware of any sounds around you, notice the presence of other people, life, and nature around you… And when you are ready, gently open your eyes again.

END

Week 4 Meditation: Transcript of the Meditation on the Breath

Please find a sitting position that is comfortable and where you can also keep your spine straight. If you can, I recommend that you sit on a chair or on a cushion with your hips higher than your knees. Balancing your spine freely without support will help you stay alert. However, if this position creates too much tension in your body, you can try to lie down or lean your back against a wall or chair. I also recommend turning off your devices and if needed, let other people know not to disturb you during the next twenty minutes.

START

For the next fifteen minutes, you are training to relax into your inherent spaciousness, to be aware of whatever arises and let it be. As sensations arise, you are invited to go to the edge and soften, experiencing and strengthening your ability to get comfortable with discomfort. For just a few minutes allow yourself the radical act of slowing down and reconnecting with a sense of ease and quiet joy.

Now, close your eyes and take one or two long, deep breaths, in through the nose and out through the mouth. If you feel tired, you can sit a little straighter, and inhale through the mouth, making it slightly longer than your exhalation. Then let your breath come naturally.

PAUSE

Bring your attention to where you most easily detect the breath, or perhaps where it's most pleasurable… It could be around your nostrils, or it could be your chest as it moves gently with each inhalation and each exhalation. For this practice, let this place be the anchor of your focus, the home base you return to when you notice your thoughts drifting.

PAUSE

Breathing in and breathing out… Notice, how you don't have to do anything, the breath naturally comes and goes, no instructions needed.

PAUSE

Each inhalation is automatically creating more space in your body and with each exhalation your body releases what it no longer needs.

PAUSE

Noticing the sensation of your breath…

PAUSE

When your mind starts to wander… just notice 'thinking' and return with your attention to where you most easily detect your breath. No need to judge, just notice with a sense of curiosity and kindness.

PAUSE

While you stay anchored in this place, broaden your attention to include your whole body. Can you find a sensation that is a little bit uncomfortable? Perhaps something is itching, your legs are feeling heavy, your stomach is grumbling… Just pick one spot to focus on.

As you focus on this unpleasant sensation, can you relax a little more?

Notice, without having to force anything, your inhalation creates more spaciousness, and each exhalation helps you to soften.

Now let the discomfort recede into the background. Is it getting less intense? Is the spaciousness getting bigger?

Just notice what comes up for you. If you don't feel anything noticeable, don't worry, simply continue focusing on your breath, holding your experience with a sense of curiosity and kindness.

PAUSE

Let's stay a few minutes with your attention on your breath.

PAUSE

Anytime your mind starts to wander, simply direct it back to your anchor.

PAUSE

Notice the beginning of your inhalation, following it all the way to the end of your exhalation.

PAUSE

Now, notice the little pause at the end or your exhalation. Rest your attention there.

PAUSE

Notice how this pause feels. Being in between two breaths; the exhalation is gone; the inhalation is not yet here. How does it feel? Is there a sense of stillness, emptiness?

Continue to rest your attention in the space between the breaths.

PAUSE

Notice how you can trust in this natural intelligence.

Notice how your breath is coming and going all by itself. Each inhalation arising out of the emptiness, each exhalation vanishing into emptiness. Bringing nourishment to your body and releasing what it no longer needs.

PAUSE

Stay with the sensation of breathing. Or, perhaps, it feels more like being breathed? Sometimes, it can feel as if life itself is breathing us.

PAUSE

And perhaps you can sense a quiet joy in feeling each new breath emerging from emptiness, vanishing into emptiness, and arising again…

PAUSE

You can trust in this natural intelligence of life. And you can trust in your ability to create spaciousness in your body and in your mind, whenever uncomfortable sensations arise.

PAUSE

Trust in this natural intelligence of life.

PAUSE

Now, slowly become aware of your surroundings again, feeling the presence of your body in the place that you are in, becoming aware of any sounds around you, noticing the presence of other people, life and nature around you… And when you are ready, you may slowly and gently open your eyes again.

END

Week 5 Meditation: Transcript of the Classic Loving-kindness Meditation

This meditation is a classic loving-kindness (mettā) mindfulness meditation. Many people have told me that this meditation was a guiding light in dark times. It can feel awkward or artificial in the beginning, but I encourage you to stick with it. In this case, you're allowed to *fake it 'til you make it.*

I also find it very effective when I am stuck in 'othering' or when something terrible happens somewhere and I can't do anything about it at the time. Sending a message of universal goodwill is at least one thing we can always do.

I first explain the technique so that you can do the meditation by yourself and adjust the words as needed.

The classic phrases are:

May I/you/they/all beings be filled with loving kindness

May I/you/they/all beings be free from inner and outer harm

May I/you/they/all beings be well in body and mind

May I/you/they/all beings be happy and at ease

You can adjust these words into your mother language and choose your own words to resonate more deeply.[108]

Then apply these phrases, in the following sequence, to: 1. a benefactor; 2. yourself; 3. someone you love; 4. a neutral person; 5. a difficult person; 6. all beings. This meditation takes 20-30 minutes.

Let's do it! I recommend turning off your devices and if needed, let other people know not to disturb you during the next thirty minutes. If you can, I recommend that you sit on a chair or on a cushion with your hips higher than your knees. Balancing your spine freely without support will help you stay alert. However, if this position creates too much tension in your body, you can try to lie down or lean your back against a wall or chair.

START

Welcome to this mettā/loving-kindness meditation to support yourself and others in difficult times, sending goodwill to all beings.

Please find a sitting position that is comfortable and where you can also keep your spine straight. When you are ready, close your eyes and take a couple deep breaths. Then let your breath come naturally.

PAUSE

Take a moment to connect with your breath. Notice where you most easily detect the breath—your nose, chest or belly, or perhaps where it's most pleasurable—and let this place be the anchor for your practice. Any time you notice your attention drifting, gently come back to your anchor.

PAUSE

Mentally scan your body and see if there are any areas of tension. Start at the top of your head, your face, noticing the area around your eyes, can you relax a little more? Notice your jaw, is it tight or resting loosely with your teeth slightly apart?

Move on to your shoulders, your chest, your arms, your hands... can you relax them a little more? If you feel tired, you can sit a little straighter at any time and take a deep inhalation and a normal exhalation.

Notice your belly, are you holding it in or is it soft, relaxed? Notice your hips, your legs, feet... feel the cushion or chair underneath you.

PAUSE

Reconnect with the sensation of your breath. Notice each inhalation and each exhalation, being fully present, right here.

PAUSE

Now, I'd like to invite you to think of a benefactor in your life. Someone you don't have an overly complicated relationship with and who gives you a sense of safety, support, kindness, love. This could be a person who has touched your life, or it could be a furry friend, such as your favorite pet. Or you may want to envision an embodiment of love and kindness, which for some people can be Buddha or Jesus or some other kind of spiritual being.

Picture this being in front of you. As you look him/her in the eyes, see how they radiate with kindness and goodwill. Their smile meets your smile. Notice how this feels in your heart-center. Stay there... The person looks at you and says:

May you be filled with loving kindness
May you be free from inner and outer harm
May you be well in body and mind
May you be happy and at ease

PAUSE

Gratefully you receive their wishes, turn around and say:

May I be filled with loving kindness
May I be free from inner and outer harm
May I be well in body and mind
May I be happy and at ease

Repeat as needed.

PAUSE

Now think of someone you love. See them in front of you. Look into their eyes and say:

May you be filled with loving kindness
May you be free from inner and outer harm
May you be well in body and mind
May you be happy and at ease

Repeat as needed

PAUSE

Now think of a neutral person. Perhaps a cashier at your local store or someone at the office. See them in front of you. Look into their eyes and say:

May you be filled with loving kindness
May you be free from inner and outer harm
May you be well in body and mind
May you be happy and at ease

PAUSE

Now think of a difficult person. It could be someone close to you that you have a difficult relationship with. Or perhaps a public figure that you cannot stand. See them in front of you. Look into their eyes and say:

May you be filled with loving kindness
May you be free from inner and outer harm
May you be well in body and mind
May you be happy and at ease

PAUSE

Finally, having all these people in mind, zoom out as if you could see the world from above, with all beings on this beautiful planet. Look at them and say:

May all beings be filled with loving kindness
May all beings be free from inner and outer harm
May all beings be well in body and mind
May all beings be happy and at ease

PAUSE

We'll stay in silence for the last few minutes of this meditation. Allow yourself to feel and bring your awareness back to your breath when your mind starts drifting.

PAUSE

Now, slowly become aware of your surroundings again. Feel your body touching the surface you are sitting on. Become aware of any sounds around you, notice the presence of other people, life, and nature around you... And when you are ready, gently open your eyes again.

END

Week 6 Meditation: Transcript of the Meditation on Resting in Open Awareness

This meditation guides you to rest in open awareness and experience a sense of openness in which all sensations arise and pass. Unlike previous meditations where you were an active observer, this one invites you to let go of that role and simply rest in awareness itself.

For some, the experience of not having an anchor in the meditation can take some getting used to, as it involves letting go of our solid sense of self. However, in my experience, this meditation becomes easier as our ability to focus the mind and remain present strengthens, which is what you have been practicing over the past weeks. I find it very effective to practice letting go and embracing emptiness, tapping into the inherent intelligence and emerging potential within. Enjoy!

Please find a sitting position that is comfortable and where you can also keep your spine straight. If you can, I recommend that you sit on a chair or on a cushion with your hips higher than your knees. Balancing your spine freely without support will help you stay alert. However, if this position creates too much tension in your body, you can try to lie down or lean your back against a wall or chair. I also recommend turning off your devices and if needed, let other people know not to disturb you during the next twenty minutes.

START

Welcome to this meditation resting in open awareness. During the next twenty minutes you are invited to let go of your focus and let your awareness be wide open. You are training to be fully present without clinging to or focusing on any experience that arises and vanishes. During this meditation you can either close your eyes or leave them open with a soft gaze into the open space, overlooking a landscape or the skyline.

PAUSE

Start by taking a couple of deep breaths... The long and deep inhalation automatically makes you more alert, while the following exhalation helps you to relax and let go. Then let your breath flow naturally, no need to direct it in any way.

PAUSE

Notice your body breathing for just a few moments. And then intentionally let go of your focus on the breath and let your awareness be wide open.

PAUSE

Notice any sounds arising, from near and far, some loud, others soft. Just listen as they arise and vanish, no need to analyze or judge, just let them come and go.

If you have your eyes open, you can do so with any images that arise, a bird flying by, a cloud changing its form.

Let your lens be soft and wide open, noticing everything and focusing on nothing.

PAUSE

Sounds and images are arising and passing in the open space of your own mind. Relax, allow everything to appear and disappear without resistance.

PAUSE

You might also notice thoughts, emotions, pictures, or words arise and pass in the open space of awareness. Pleasant or unpleasant, like the sounds, allow any thoughts, emotions and sensations to appear and disappear, without struggle or resistance.

PAUSE

Notice how there is also spaciousness in your body. Sensations, pleasant and unpleasant, are coming and going. Your heart beating, your blood flowing, and your breath moving in and out like a breeze. Everything is in constant motion, arising and passing in open awareness.

PAUSE

Let your mind be wide like the sky. If it is helpful, you can use an image; like traveling along the open sky above the sea or the ever-expanding universe…

Let this spacious, open awareness be all around you.

PAUSE

Notice how there is no end to awareness.

Just openness, spaciousness, in which different forms arise and vanish again.

PAUSE

Experiencing life as it unfolds, you are resting in awareness itself.

PAUSE

Allow yourself to rest in awareness.

PAUSE

Awareness is vast like the sky. Perhaps you can sense the qualities of awareness itself: expansive, clear, peaceful, empty and full of potential.

PAUSE

Expansive, clear, peaceful, and empty and full of potential.

PAUSE

You are awareness expressing itself.

PAUSE

Stay here in silence for a little longer. Fully alert and fully relaxed.

PAUSE

Now, slowly become aware of your surroundings again, feeling the presence of your body in the place that you are in, becoming aware of any sounds around you, noticing the presence of other people, life and nature around you… And when you are ready, if you had your eyes closed, you may slowly and gently open them again.

END

Endnotes

(All urls accessed July 2024)

[1] The number of weather-related disasters has increased by a factor of five from 1970 to 2019. Pavlinovic, D. (2021) "Climate and weather related disasters surge five-fold over 50 years, but early warnings save lives - WMO report" *UN News, Climate and Environment* (1 Sept.). tinyurl.com/conscious006

[2] Esper, J., Torbenson, M. (2024) "2023 summer warmth unparalleled over the past 2,000 years", *Nature*, 2024. tinyurl.com/conscious005

[3] For more information on planetary boundaries, I recommend both *10 years to transform the future of humanity – or destabilize the planet* (10 October 2020) Johann Rockström [TED video] Countdown Global Launch. tinyurl.com/conscious003 and *Breaking boundaries: the science of our planet* (2021) [Netflix].

[4] World Wildlife Fund for Nature (undated) "What is the sixth mass extinction and what can we do about it?" *WWF website.* tinyurl.com/conscious001

[5]FAO, IFAD, UNICEF, WFP and WHO. (2024) *The State of Food Security and Nutrition in the World 2024 – Financing to end hunger, food insecurity and malnutrition in all its forms.* Rome. https://doi.org/10.4060/cd1254en

[6] Persson, L. *et al.* (2022) "Outside the safe operating space of planetary boundary for novel entities", *Environmental Science and Technology*, 56(3), pp. 1510–1521. tinyurl.com/conscious007

[7] Oceana (undated) "Plastic pollution—tackling the plastics crisis at the source", *Oceana website.* tinyurl.com/conscious002

[8] Carrington, D. (2022) "Microplastics found in human blood for the first time," *The Guardian*, 24 March 2022. tinyurl.com/conscious004

[9] Moss, J. (2021) *The Burnout Epidemic: The Rise of Chronic Stress and How We Can Fix It.* Boston: Harvard Business Review Press.

[10] Hertz, N. (2021) *The Lonely Century: How to Restore Human Connection in a World That's Pulling Apart.* New York: Currency

[11] Thiagarajan, T. and Newson, J. (4 March 2024) The Mental State of the World in 2023: A Perspective on Internet-Enabled Populations. The Global Mind Project. tinyurl.com/conscious040

[12] World Health Organization (17 November 2021) "Adolescent mental health". tinyurl.com/conscious009

[13] Hickman, C. et al. (2021) "Climate anxiety in children and young people and their beliefs about government responses to climate change: a global survey", *Lancet Planetary Health* 5(12) e863-e873. tinyurl.com/conscious031

[14] Haidt, J. (2024) *The Anxious Generation: How the Great Rewiring of Childhood Is Causing an Epidemic of Mental Illness.* p. 38. New York: Penguin Press.

[15] Pinker, S. (2019) *Enlightenment Now: The Case for Reason, Science, Humanism and Progress.* London: Penguin Random House.

[16] "In central Asia and Europe anthropologists have discovered archeological evidence, dating back to around 10,000 years ago (8000 BC), that indicate *Homo sapiens* lived rather peacefully in egalitarian communities, with a close sense of community where males and females were valued equally. … During this epoch, humans lived in close proximity with wild, undomesticated nature and appreciated a strong sense of connection with the living Earth." Hutchins, G. and Storm, L. (2019) *Regenerative Leadership: The DNA of life-affirming 21st century organizations.* p. 4. Kent: Wordzworth Publishing.

[17] "Don't believe tree-huggers who claim that our ancestors lived in harmony with nature. Long before the Industrial Revolution, *Homo sapiens* held the record among all organisms for driving the most plant and animal species to their extinctions. We have the dubious distinction of being the deadliest species in the annals of biology." Harari, Y. N. (2015) *Sapiens: A Brief History of Humankind.* p. 82. London: Vintage.

[18] See, for example: Bregman, R. (2020) *Humankind: A Hopeful History.* London: Bloomsbury Publishing.

[19] Harari, Y.N. (2015) *Sapiens: A Brief History of Humankind.* New York: Harper Perennial.

[20] Ostrom, E. (2009) 'Beyond markets and states: Polycentric governance of complex economic systems' [Lecture] Nobel Prize. 8 December. tinyurl.com/conscious008

[21]United Nations Human Development Report (2020) "The next frontier: Human development and the Anthropocene". tinyurl.com/conscious032

[22] Hutchins, G. and Storm, L. (2019) *Regenerative Leadership: The DNA of life-affirming 21st century organizations.* Kent: Wordzworth Publishing.

[23] Hawken, P. (2021) *Regeneration: Ending the Climate Crisis in One Generation.* London: Penguin Books.

[24] Scharmer, O. and Kaeufer, K. (2013) *Leading from the Emerging Future: From Ego-System to Eco-System Economies.* p. 20. San Francisco: Berret-Koehler Publishers, Inc.

[25] Note that the programs' names may change as programs are integrated somewhere else or replaced by new ones.

[26] Goleman, D. and Davidson, R.J. (2018) *Altered Traits: Science Reveals How Meditation Changes Your Mind, Brain and Body.* New York: Penguin Random House.

[27] Smith, J.A, et al. (2017) "The state of mindfulness science" *The Greater Good Magazine.* tinyurl.com/conscious010

[28] Thích Nhất Hạnh (2015) *The Power of Quiet in a World Full of Noise.* p. 99. London: Penguin Random House.

[29] Inspired by a talk by Pema Chödrön: "You could ask what would be a good use of my life, thinking the answer is going to be a career choice or something, but I would say the most important thing is using your life to train in being present—in being here with an open heart. Synchronizing your mind with your body—having them be in the same place at the same time with a brave, honest, but also gentle attitude towards yourself and towards what you see." Gimian, C.R. (2012) *Smile at Fear: A Retreat with Pema Chödrön.* Boulder, Colorado: Shambhala Publications.

[30] Griffey, H. (2018) "The lost art of concentration: being distracted in a digital world", *The Guardian*, 14 October.

[31] Hari, J. (2022) *Stolen Focus: Why You Can't Pay Attention—and How to Think Deeply Again.* New York: Crown.

[32] Recent research found even a moderate increase in adult's ability to concentrate over the last three decades. Andrzejewski, D. *et al.* (2024) "Is there a Flynn effect for attention? Cross-temporal meta analytical evidence for better test performance (1990-2021)". *Personality and Individual Preferences*, Vol 2016, January. tinyurl.com/conscious035

[33] See research by psychiatrist and neuroscientist Judson Brewer, MD, PhD. Books: Brewer, J. (2017) *The Craving Mind: From Cigarettes to Smartphones to Love—Why We Get Hooked and How We Can Break Bad Habits*. New Haven: Yale University Press. Brewer, J. (2021) *Unwinding Anxiety: New Science Shows How to Break the Cycles of Worry and Fear to Heal Your Mind*. New York: Avery.

[34] *How Silence can lead us to a sustainable world* (2019) Laura Storm [TEDx film]. Hamburg, Germany. tinyurl.com/conscious033

[35] Zorn, J. and Marz, L. (2022) *Golden: The Power of Silence in a World full of Noise*. London: Penguin Random House.

[36] Justin Zorn and Leigh Marz (2017) "The busier you are, the more you need quiet time" *Harvard Business Review*. March 17. tinyurl.com/conscious030

[37] Thích Nhất Hạnh (2015) *The Power of Quiet in a World Full of Noise*. London: Penguin Random House.

[38] Goleman, D. and Davidson, R.J. (2018) *Altered Traits: Science Reveals How Meditation Changes Your Mind, Brain and Body*. New York: Penguin Random House.

[39] The neuroscientist and Professor in Psychology Dr Amishi P. Jha and her team found that meditating for 12 minutes, 5 times a week seems to be the most effective time for you to improve your concentration and be present during your day. The benefit is additive, the more you practice, the greater the benefit. Jha, A.P. (2021) *Peak Mind: 12 minutes a day to find your focus, meet the challenge and be fully present when it matters most*. London: Piatkus.

[40] Note that the window of tolerance can be quite different for different people. For example, Highly Sensitive People are likely to have a narrower window of tolerance as their nervous system is more sensitive and reactive. Another example is neurodivergent people who tend to have more rigid nervous systems and narrower windows of tolerance. See Neff, Megan Anna. (no date) "The Autistic and ADHD Nervous

System" *Neurodivergent Insights.* tinyurl.com/conscious011 Also, Passaler, Linnea. (2023) "What Is a Highly Sensitive Person?" *Heal Your Nervous System.* 6 April. tinyurl.com/conscious012

[41] Siegel, D. (2011) *Mindsight: Transform Your Brain with the New Science of Kindness.* London: Oneworld.

[42] For a detailed explanation of the connection between breathwork, the vagus nerve, the heart and the brain, I recommend Chapter Four: McKeown, P. (2021) *The Breathing Cure: Exercises to Develop New Breathing Habits for a Healthier, Happier and Longer Life.* Moycullen: OxyAt Books.

[43] While the definite primary source is unclear, Albert Einstein may have said: "A human being is a part of the whole called by us universe, a part limited in time and space. He experiences himself, his thoughts and feeling as something separated from the rest, a kind of optical delusion of his consciousness. This delusion is a kind of prison for us, restricting us to our personal desires and to affection for a few persons nearest to us. Our task must be to free ourselves from this prison by widening our circle of compassion to embrace all living creatures and the whole of nature in its beauty."

[44] Attributed to the teachings of Zen Master Thích Nhất Hạnh.

[45] Levine, P. A. (2008) *Healing Trauma: A Pioneering Program for Restoring the Wisdom of Your Body.* Boulder, Colorado: Sounds True.

[46] Maté, G. and Maté, D. (2022) *The Myth of Normal: Trauma, Illness, and Healing in a Toxic Culture.* p. 45. London: Penguin Random House.

[47] US Department of Health & Human Services, Administration for Children and Families, Administration on Children, Youth and Families, Children's Bureau (2023) *Child maltreatment 2021.* Washington, DC. tinyurl.com/conscious023

[48] BBC (2019) *Can the legacy of trauma be passed down the generations?* tinyurl.com/conscious024

[49] Klosin, A. *et al.* (2017) "Transgenerational transmission of environmental information in C. elegans", *Science* 356 pp. 320-323. tinyurl.com/conscious025

[50] Maté, G. and Maté, D. (2022) *The Myth of Normal: Trauma, Illness, and Healing in a Toxic Culture.* p. 32. London: Penguin Random House.

[51] van der Kolk, B. (2014) *The Body Keeps the Score: Mind, Brain and Body in the Transformation of Trauma.* London: Penguin Random House.

[52] Polman, P. and Winston, A. S. (2021) *Net positive: How Courageous Companies Thrive by Giving More Than They Take*. Boston: Harvard Business Review Press.

[53] Hawken, P. (2021) *Regeneration: Ending the Climate Crisis in One Generation.* New York: Penguin Books.

[54] Wahl, D.C. (2016) *Designing Regenerative Cultures.* Axminster: Triarchy Press.

[55] Hutchins, G. and Storm, L. (2019) *Regenerative Leadership: The DNA of life-affirming 21st century organizations.* Kent: Wordzworth Publishing.

[56] Lovins, H., Wallis, S., Wijkman, A. and Fullerton, J. (2018) *A Finer Future: Creating an Economy in Service to Life*. Canada: New Society Publishers.

[57] Fullerton, J. (2015) "White Paper: Regenerative Capitalism: How universal principles and patterns will shape our new economy". Capital Institute. April 21. tinyurl.com/conscious013

[58] *Kiss the Ground* (2020) Josh Tickell [Film]. Tribeca Film Festival: Big Picture Ranch. https://kissthegroundmovie.com/

[59]Wikipedia (no date) *Patagonia Inc.* tinyurl.com/conscious041

[60] Dunkley, E. and Jones, G. (2022) "Patagonia founder hands company trust to tackle climate crisis", *Financial Times*, 15 September. tinyurl.com/conscious014 (Subscription only).

[61] Aratani, L. (2023) "We've lost the right to be pessimistic: Patagonia treads fine line tackling climate crisis as for-profit company", *The Guardian*, March 12. tinyurl.com/conscious026 (Subscription only).

[62] Wahl, D.C. (2016) *Designing Regenerative Cultures.* p. 45. Axminster: Triarchy Press.

[63] Emotions are deeply integrated into the brain's neural circuitry, particularly in the limbic system, which governs emotional responses. Thinking and feeling cannot be separated and are hence part of the mind. For an introduction to the subject of emotions and the brain I recommend: Goleman, D. (2020) *Emotional Intelligence: Why it can matter more than IQ.* London: Bloomsbury Publishing.

[64] If you are interested in learning more about these personality types, I recommend Kornfield, J. (2009) Chapter 12 "Buddhist Personality Types," *The Wise Heart: A Guide to the Universal Teachings of Buddhist Psychology*. New York: Bantam Books (Paperback Edition).

[65] The phrase "no mud, no lotus" comes from Buddhist philosophy, attributed to Zen Master Thích Nhất Hạnh. This saying encapsulates a significant principle of Buddhism, emphasizing the necessity of suffering as a precursor to understanding, enlightenment, and joy.

[66] David, S. (2021) [X, formerly Twitter] 14 Jan. tinyurl.com/conscious015

[67] Brown, B. (2015) *Daring Greatly: How the Courage to Be Vulnerable Transforms the Way We Live, Love, Parent, and Lead.* London: Penguin Life.

[68] If you would like further information on this, I recommend reading Hari, J. (2019) *Lost Connections: Why You're Depressed and How to Find Hope.* London: Bloomsbury.

[69] For example, if you decided to lose weight and after a hard day you finish the whole pot of ice cream, does shame help you not to do it next time? No, it makes you feel worse. Research shows what helps to break negative habit loops is compassion and mindfulness of our feelings and needs before we eat the ice cream, drink, smoke, binge watch, etc. See Brewer, J. (2017) *The Craving Mind: From Cigarettes to Smartphones to Love—Why We Get Hooked and How We Can Break Bad Habits.* New Haven: Yale University Press.

[70] Brach, T. (2013) Chapter Eight "Investigating Core Beliefs", *True Refuge: Finding Peace and Freedom in Your Own Awakened Heart.* London: Hay House.

[71] Katie, B. with Mitchell, S. (2002) *Loving What Is: Four questions that can change your life.* New York: Harmony Books.

[72] Writing your answers down improves our ability to process and remember the information. Some research indicated that writing by hand rather than using a keyboard may be even more impactful. Frontiers (2024) "Writing by hand may increase brain connectivity more than typing on a keyboard" 26 January. tinyurl.com/conscious017

[73] "Go to the edge and soften" is attributed to the Tibetan teacher Chögyam Trungpa

[74] Maconachie, R. (2024) "'*We Miners die a lot.*' Appalling conditions and poverty wages: the lives of cobalt miners in DRC", *The Conversation* (January 30). tinyurl.com/conscious028

[75] Figueres, C. and Rivett-Carnac, T. (2020) *The Future We Choose: The Stubborn Optimist's Guide to the Climate Crisis.* p. 57. Manila Press.

[76] Interview with Christiana Figueres and Tom Rivett-Carnac by Sam Mowe (2020). "The future we choose: The chief architects of the Paris Agreement say it's up to all of us to save the planet", *TRICYCLE The Buddhist Review*. (3 August) tinyurl.com/conscious021(Subscription only).

[77] Figueres, C. and Rivett-Carnac, T. (2020) *The Future We Choose: The Stubborn Optimist's Guide to the Climate Crisis.* London: Manila Press.

[78] Interview with Brené Brown by Dan Schwabel (2013) "Brene Brown: How vulnerability Can Make Our Lives Better" *Forbes*, 21 April. tinyurl.com/conscious036

[79] Dethmer, J., Chaman, D., and Klemp, K. W. (2014) identify four ways of leading: "To Me" (life happens to me), "By Me" (I make life happen), "Through Me" (I cooperate with life happening), and "As Me" (life is me), moving from a state of separateness to responsibility, to surrender, and to oneness. *The 15 Commitments of Conscious Leadership: A new paradigm for sustainable success.* 1st edn. Dethmer, Chapman & Klemp

[80] Figueres, C. (2020) *The case for stubborn optimism on climate.* tinyurl.com/conscious018

[81] Sarah Ichioka and Michael Pawlyn introduce the concept of *Possibilism* as an alternative to the somewhat fatalist connotation of optimism or pessimism. Possibilism combines evidence-gathering, design for uncertainty, and agency expansion. Ichioka, S. and Pawlyn, M (2021) *Flourish: Design Paradigms for Our Planetary Emergency.* Axminster: Triarchy Press.

[82] Goodall, J. and Abrams, D (2021) *The Book of Hope: A Survival Guide for Trying Times.* New York: MacMillan.

[83] Kornfield, J. (2009) *The Wise Heart: A Guide to the Universal Teachings of Buddhist Psychology*. p. 350-351. New York: Bantam Books.

[84] Childre, D., Martin, H., and Beech, D. (2000) *The HeartMath Solution: The Institute of HeartMath's Revolutionary Program for Engaging the Power of the Heart's Intelligence.* San Francisco: Harper One.

[85] "When we let thoughts come and go without clinging, we can use thought, but we rest in the heart." Kornfield, J. (2009) *The Wise Heart: A Guide to the Universal Teachings of Buddhist Psychology*. p. 147. New York: Bantam Books (Paperback Edition).

[86] Ibid. p. 386.

[87] For example, 442 Central (2023) *Jack Grealish the gentle soul.* tinyurl.com/conscious019

[88] Bregman, R. (2020) *Humankind: A Hopeful History*. London: Bloomsbury Publishing.

[89] Keltner, D. (2012) "The Compassionate Species," *The Greater Good Magazine: Science Based Insights for a Meaningful Life* (July 31) tinyurl.com/conscious037

[90] Darwin, C. (1871), as quoted in in Feldman, C. and Kuyken, W (2019) *Mindfulness: Ancients Wisdom Meets Modern Psychology*. p. 154. New York: Guilford Press.

[91] Cited in Baraz, J. and Alexander, S. (2012) *Awakening Joy: 10 Steps to Happiness*. p. 71. Berkeley: Parallax Press.

[92] The Pema Chödrön Foundation (no date) *Awakening Compassion* Available for purchase at: tinyurl.com/conscious038

[93]American Psychological Association (2011) *Building Resilience* (11 April) Washington DC: APA. tinyurl.com/conscious022

[94] Lewis, S.E. (2013) "Trauma and the making of flexible minds in the Tibetan exile community" *Ethos* 41(3), pp. 313–336. tinyurl.com/conscious034

[95] Hanson, R. (2018) *Resilient: Find Your Inner Strength*. p. 2. London: Penguin Random House.

[96] Hanson, R. with Mendius, R. (2009) *Buddha's Brain: The Practical Neuroscience of Happiness, Love and Wisdom*. Oakland: Harbinger Publications.

[97] Friedman, M. (1970) "A Friedman doctrine—the social responsibility of business is to increase its profits" *The New York Times*, 13 September. Subscription only: tinyurl.com/conscious029

[98] Schwab, K. (2019) "Davos Manifesto 2020: The universal purpose of a company in the fourth industrial revolution", *World Economic Forum*, 2 December. tinyurl.com/conscious016

[99] Deloitte (2024) *2024 Gen Z and Millennial Survey: Living and working with purpose in a transforming world.* tinyurl.com/conscious039

[100] Sinek, S. (2009). *Start with Why: How Great Leaders Inspire Everyone to Take Action.* p. 39. New York: Penguin.

[101] Grant, A., his study cited in Esfahani Smith, E. (2017) *The Power of Meaning: The True Route to Happiness,* p. 93. London: Penguin.

[102] Duckworth, A. (2017) *Grit: Why Passion and Resilience are the Secrets to Success,* pp. 180-181. London: Penguin. (Published in New York in 2016, by Scribner, as *Grit: The Power of Passion and Perseverance.*)

[103] Clear, J. (2024) "Let your values drive your choices" (no date). https://jamesclear.com/values-choices

[104] Grant, A. (2021) *Think Again: The Power of Knowing What You Don't Know,* p. 240. London: WH Allen.

[105] Ibid. p. 241.

[106] Echoing the saying popularly attributed to Albert Einstein, "the more I learn, the more I realize how much I don't know."

[107] "When a complex system is far from equilibrium, small islands of coherence in a sea of chaos have the capacity to shift the entire system to a higher order." Ilya Prigogine, Nobel Prize-winning chemist, quoted by: Stephen Posner (2023) "Islands of coherence", Garrison Institute, 14 July. tinyurl.com/conscious020

[108] For example, I've been using: *May I/you/they be happy. May I/you/they be safe. May I/you/their body be healthy and strong. May my/your/their mind be peaceful. And may my/your/their heart be full of love.* Especially if the traditional words feel strange, try your own!

ACKNOWLEDGMENTS

This book is the culmination of countless moments of insight, support, and encouragement from many wonderful people in my life, for whom I am profoundly grateful.

Firstly, a special thanks to my husband, Reto, for his enduring love and unwavering support of my work. Your presence is a constant source of strength and joy in my life. To my children, thank you for filling our home with laughter and reminding me every day of the importance of play. May this book serve your and future generations.

I am indebted to my parents and ancestors, without whom my life would not have been possible. Thank you for the foundation you have given me. I owe a profound debt of gratitude to all teachers who have brought the wisdom of the Buddhist dharma teachings to the West. Special thanks to Jack Kornfield, Tara Brach, and Lama Tilmann Lhündrup for their direct guidance and to the late Zen Master Thích Nhất Hạnh, whose teachings have deeply influenced my thinking, even from afar. I extend my sincere gratitude to all the authors and individuals mentioned in this book. Your insights and contributions have profoundly informed and enriched my thinking.

A special note of appreciation to my publisher, Andrew Carey from Triarchy Press, for believing in this book and your dedication to bringing it to life in the best possible way. Your insights have been instrumental in shaping this project, and I am profoundly grateful for your guidance and commitment. I am incredibly grateful to Sarah Ichioka for making this vital introduction. Thank you, Jennie Nash, for your early coaching on my idea and to Barbara Boyd for your valuable feedback on my work. Ruth Bullivant, your editing skills were matched only by your humor and patience. Charline Catteeuw, thank you for lending your graphic design expertise to bring clarity and elegance to my ideas.

My journey has been immeasurably enriched by the founders of The Klosters Forum, who introduced me to the world of regenerative thinking and a network of inspiring changemakers. Thank you for inviting me into this dedicated organization. To my spiritual friends—Constanze, Daniela, Sabine, Sarah, and Helga—thank you for being the catalysts to my teaching. Your friendship, shared insights, and encouragement have been a source of motivation on this path.

To everyone on this shared journey of creating meaningful change and honoring our interbeing with each other, all living beings, and this planet—my deepest thanks. Your courage and commitment inspire me every day.

About the Author

Susanne von der Becke is the founder of VDB Insights, where she supports changemakers in their journeys to create social and environmental impact through mindfulness-based workshops and retreats. A former investment banker with extensive experience as an active investor and board member, she applies her expertise in finance and leadership to drive meaningful change.

Susanne is an alumna of Harvard Business School, holds a Ph.D. in Science from ETH Zurich, and degrees from The London School of Economics and Political Science. She is a certified Mindfulness Meditation Teacher, trained by Jack Kornfield and Tara Brach, and accredited by the Greater Good Science Center at UC Berkeley. Additionally, she is a certified Breath Coach, using transformational breath journeys to accelerate inner transformation for greater wellbeing and effective leadership.

Previously serving as the Chairwoman of The Klosters Forum, Susanne has been actively involved in environmental advocacy for many years. In 2015, she was honored as a "Rising Talent" by the Women's Forum for the Economy & Society, recognizing her contributions to fostering impactful change.

www.susannevonderbecke.com

ABOUT THE PUBLISHER

Triarchy Press is an independent publisher of books that bring a wider, systemic or contextual approach to many different areas of life, including:

Government, Education, Health and other public services
Ecology, Sustainability and Regenerative Cultures
Leading and Managing Organizations
Psychotherapy and Arts and other Expressive Therapies
The Money System
Walking, Psychogeography and Mythogeography
Movement and Somatics
Innovation
The Future and Future Studies

For books by Barry Oshry, John Seddon, Nora Bateson, Gregory Bateson, Daniel Wahl, Andy Hines, Miranda Tufnell, Russ Ackoff, Phil Smith, Lucy Neal, Patricia Lustig, Claire Loussouarn, Linda Hartley, Bill Tate, Sandra Reeve, Graham Leicester, May East, Alyson Hallett, Nelisha Wickremasinghe and many other remarkable writers, please visit:

www.triarchypress.net